MathFlare

Name: _______________________

Class: __________

Teacher: ___________________

Introduction

As parents and educators, we recognize the pivotal role mathematics plays in shaping a child's academic journey and future success. Yet, the path to mathematical proficiency can often seem daunting, fraught with challenges and complexities. That's where the transformative power of MathFlare Workbooks shine through, illuminating the way forward with clarity, precision, and purpose.

Introducing MathFlare Workbooks – a beacon of guidance, a testament to excellence, and a catalyst for achievement. Crafted with meticulous care and expertise, MathFlare Workbooks stand as paragons of educational excellence, designed to nurture young minds, ignite a passion for learning, and develop a deep-rooted understanding of mathematical concepts.

Picture this: your child eagerly delves into the pages of Mathflare Workbook, greeted by a step-by-step guide illuminated with vivid examples that demystify complex mathematical concepts. With each turn of the page, they embark on a journey of discovery, encountering thoughtfully curated practice questions that reinforce learning and hone problem-solving skills. And when they unveil the answers to those very questions, a sense of accomplishment blossoms within them – a tangible reward for their hard work and dedication.

But MathFlare Workbooks are more than just tools for learning; they are pathways to comprehension, fostering a deep-seated understanding of mathematical concepts through a sequential, logical flow. From fundamental principles to advanced problem-solving strategies, every chapter builds upon the last, ensuring a robust foundation upon which future knowledge can be constructed.

As parents, we yearn for nothing more than to see our children thrive, to witness the spark of inspiration ignited within them as they conquer academic challenges with confidence and poise. MathFlare Workbooks serve as partners in this noble endeavor, offering not just practice questions, but the keys to unlocking a world of opportunity.

And for teachers, MathFlare Workbooks stand as invaluable allies in the quest to cultivate mathematical proficiency in the classroom. With answers readily available, instructors can focus on guiding and nurturing their students, confident in the knowledge that MathFlare Workbooks provide a solid framework upon which to build.

In the pages of MathFlare Workbooks, we find not just the promise of academic excellence, but the seeds of a brighter tomorrow. So let us embrace the power of mathematics, let us champion the journey of learning, and let us pave the way for a generation of young minds poised to shape the world. With MathFlare Workbooks as our guide, the possibilities are infinite, and the future, bright.

Table of Contents

MathFlare
Grade 2
MATH WORKBOOK
Step by Step Guide and Essential Practice with Answers
Addition Subtraction
Multiplication
Place Value and Expanded Notations
Geometry
MathFlare Publishing

MathFlare
Grade 2-3
MATH WORKBOOK
Step by Step Guide and Essential Practice with Answers
Addition Subtraction
Multiplication and Division
Place Value and Expanded Notations
Geometry
MathFlare Publishing

MathFlare
Grade 3
MATH WORKBOOK
Step by Step Guide and Essential Practice with Answers
Multiplication and Division
Decimals
Place Value and Expanded Notations
Fractions and Geometry
MathFlare Publishing

MathFlare
Grade 1
MATH WORKBOOK
Step by Step Guide and Essential Practice with Answers
Counting and Numbers
Addition and Subtraction
Place Value and Expanded Notations
Understanding Time
MathFlare Publishing

MathFlare
Grade 1-2
MATH WORKBOOK
Step by Step Guide and Essential Practice with Answers
Counting and Numbers
Addition and Subtraction
Place Value and Expanded Notations
Understanding Time
MathFlare Publishing

MathFlare
Grade 3-4
MATH WORKBOOK
Step by Step Guide and Essential Practice with Answers
Addition Subtraction
Multiplication Division
Place Value and Expanded Notations
Fractions and Geometry
MathFlare Publishing

MathFlare
Grade 4
MATH WORKBOOK
Step by Step Guide and Essential Practice with Answers
Addition Subtraction
Multiplication Division
Place Value and Expanded Notations
Fractions and Geometry
MathFlare Publishing

MathFlare
Grade 4-5
MATH WORKBOOK
Step by Step Guide and Essential Practice with Answers
Multiplication Division
Place Value and Expanded Notations
Fractions and Geometry
Unit Conversion
MathFlare Publishing

MathFlare
Grade 5
MATH WORKBOOK
Step by Step Guide and Essential Practice with Answers
Multiplication Division
Place Value and Expanded Notations
Fractions and Geometry
Unit Conversion
MathFlare Publishing

MathFlare
Grade 5-6
MATH WORKBOOK
Step by Step Guide and Essential Practice with Answers
Multiplication Division
Place Value and Expanded Notations
Fractions and Geometry
Units and Statistics
MathFlare Publishing

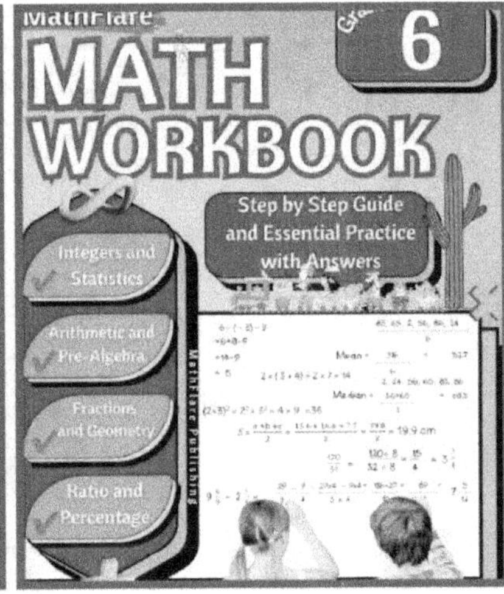
MathFlare
Grade 6
MATH WORKBOOK
Step by Step Guide and Essential Practice with Answers
Integers and Statistics
Arithmetic and Pre-Algebra
Fractions and Geometry
Ratio and Percentage
MathFlare Publishing

MathFlare
Grade 6-7
MATH WORKBOOK
Step by Step Guide and Essential Practice with Answers
Arithmetic and Pre-Algebra
Ratio, Percent Proportion
Geometry
Statistics
MathFlare Publishing

MathFlare
Grade 7
MATH WORKBOOK
Step by Step Guide and Essential Practice with Answers
Pre-Algebra
Ratio, Percent Proportion
Geometry
Statistics
MathFlare Publishing

MathFlare
Grade 7-8
MATH WORKBOOK
Step by Step Guide and Essential Practice with Answers
Pre-Algebra
Ratio, Percent Proportion
Geometry and Cartesian Plane
Statistics
MathFlare Publishing

MathFlare
Grade 8-9
MATH WORKBOOK
Step by Step Guide and Essential Practice with Answers
Pre-Algebra
Ratio, Proportion and Percentage
Linear Equations
Geometry and Cartesian Plane
MathFlare Publishing

MathFlare
Grade 8
MATH WORKBOOK
Step by Step Guide and Essential Practice with Answers
Pre-Algebra
Percentage
Linear Equations
Geometry
MathFlare Publishing

Equations and Expressions

Solving One-Step Equations

Solving one-step equations involves finding the value of the variable that makes the equation true. In a one-step equation, there is only one operation (addition, subtraction, multiplication, or division) performed on the variable.

The goal is to isolate the variable on one side of the equation by performing inverse operations.

For example:

Given the equation $6 = -3z$, where we want to solve for z.

The given equation is already in the form of a one-step equation, with z being multiplied by -3.

To isolate z, we need to perform the inverse operation of multiplication, which is division.

Divide both sides by -3:

$$\frac{6}{-3} = \frac{-3z}{-3}$$

Simplify:

$$-2 = z$$

So, the solution to the equation is $z = -2$.

When we substitute the value of $z = -2$ back into the original equation, $6 = -3(-2)$, it simplifies to $6 = 6$. This confirms that our solution is correct because it satisfies the original equation.

Solving Two-Step Equations

Solving two-step equations involves finding the value of the variable that makes the equation true. In a two-step equation, two operations (addition, subtraction, multiplication, or division) are performed on the variable.

The goal is to isolate the variable on one side of the equation by performing inverse operations in the reverse order of operations.

For example:

Given the equation $18 = (10 + b) - 2$, where we want to solve for b.

To solve for b, we need to undo the operations that have been performed on b.

1. Undo the subtraction by adding 2 to both sides:

$$18 + 2 = (10 + b) - 2 + 2$$

$$20 = 10 + b$$

2. Undo the addition by subtracting 10 from both sides:

$$20 - 10 = 10 + b - 10$$

$$10 = b$$

So, the solution to the equation is $b = 10$

Let's substitute $b = 10$ back into the original equation to verify if it satisfies the equation:

Original equation:

$$18 = (10 + b) - 2:$$

Substitute b = 10:

$$18 = (10 + 10) - 2$$

simplify:

$$18 = 20 - 2$$

$$18 = 18$$

Since the equation simplifies to 18 =18, it confirms that our solution b = 10 is correct.

<u>Solving Multi-Step Equations</u>

Solving multi-step equations involves finding the value of the variable that makes the equation true. In a multi-step equation, multiple operations (addition, subtraction, multiplication, or division) are performed on the variable.

The goal is to isolate the variable on one side of the equation by performing inverse operations in the reverse order of operations.

Example:

Given the equation $-3m - m = -8$, where we want to solve for m.

To solve for m, we need to undo the operations that have been performed on m.

1. Combine like terms on the left side:

$$-3m - m = -4m$$

2. Substitute the combined term back into the equation:

$$-4m = -8$$

3. Undo the multiplication by dividing both sides by $-4-4$:

$$\frac{-4m}{-4} = \frac{-8}{-4}$$

$$m = 2$$

Let's substitute m = 2 back into the original equation to verify if it satisfies the equation:

Original equation:

$$-3m - m = -8$$

Substitute m = 2:

$$-3(2) - 2 = -8$$

simplify:

$$-6 - 2 = -8$$

$$-8 = -8$$

Since the equation simplifies to 8 = 8, it confirms that our solution m = 2 is correct.

Solving Equations (One Side)

Solving one-step equations involves performing a single operation to isolate the variable and find its value.

Let's solve an equation step by step: 16 + x = 31

1. **Identify the Goal:**

    The goal is to isolate the variable x on one side of the equation.

2. **Simplify the Equation:** Combine like terms on both sides of the equation, if necessary.

    The equation is already simplified.

3. **Undo Addition or Subtraction:** If there's addition or subtraction involving the variable, undo it by performing the opposite operation on both sides of the equation.

Since x is being added to 16, we'll undo this operation by subtracting 16 from both sides of the equation:

$$16 + x - 16 = 31 - 16$$

4. **Isolate the Variable**: Ensure that the variable is alone on one side of the equation.

$$x = 15$$

5. **Check Your Solution**: Substitute the value of x back into the original equation to verify that it satisfies the equation.

$$16 + 15 = 31$$

$$31 = 31$$

The equation is balanced.

Equations (Two Sides)

A two-sided equation is an equation where both sides have expressions with variables and constants. The goal when solving a two-sided equation is to find the value of the variable that makes both sides equal.

For example: Let's solve an equation:

$$9 + 8x + 8 = 64 + x + 2$$

-   **Combine Like Terms**: Simplify each side of the equation by combining like terms (terms with the same variable or constants).

$$9 + 8x + 8 = 64 + x + 2$$

$$17 + 8x = 66 + x$$

-   **Isolate the Variable**: Use inverse operations to isolate the variable on one side of the equation.

subtract x from both sides:

$$17 + 8x - x = 66 + x - x$$

$$17 + 7x = 66$$

subtracting 17 from both sides:

$$17 - 17 + 7x = 66 - 17$$

$$7x = 49$$

divide both sides by 7:

$$\frac{7x}{7} = \frac{49}{7} = x = 7$$

- **Check Solution:** Once you find the solution, substitute it back into the original equation to ensure it makes the equation true.

Substitute $x = 7$ back into the original equation:

$$9 + 8(7) + 8 = 64 + 7 + 2$$

$$9 + 56 + 8 = 64 + 7 + 2$$

$$73 = 73$$

Combining and Distributing Terms

The distributive property is a fundamental concept in algebra that helps simplify expressions by distributing terms. Understanding the distributive property is essential for simplifying, factoring, expanding expressions and solving equations in algebra.

The distributive property states that for any numbers a, b, and c, the expression $a \times (b+c)$ is equal to $a \times b + a \times c$. In other words, we can distribute the term a across the terms inside the parentheses.

Combining and Distributing Terms:

1. **Combining Like Terms:** Combining like terms involves adding or subtracting terms that have the same variable and exponent.

2. **Distributing Terms:** Distributing terms involves multiplying a term outside parentheses by each term inside the parentheses.

Let's solve some examples:

1. **Combining Like Terms:** $-6m + 6m$

   The terms $-6m$ and $6m$ cancel each other out, resulting in 0.

   $$-6m + 6m = 0$$

2. **Distributing Terms:** $-7(8x + 7) - 3(2 - 7x)$

   Distribute -7 and -3 across the terms inside the parentheses:

   $$-7 \times 8x - 7 \times 7 - 3 \times 2 + 3 \times 7x$$

   $$-56x - 49 - 6 + 21x$$

   Combine like terms:

$$-56x + 21x - 49 - 6$$

$$-35x - 55$$

3. **Combining and Distributing Terms:** $(1 + 6m) \times -5 - 3(3m + 2)$

Distribute -5 and -3 across the terms inside the parentheses:

$$-5 \times 1 - 5 \times 6m - 3 \times 3m - 3 \times 2$$

$$-5 - 30m - 9m - 6$$

Combine like terms:

$$-5 - 36m - 6$$

$$-36m - 11$$

Factoring with Special Cases

Factoring is the process of expressing a polynomial as the product of its factors. It is a fundamental skill in algebra used to simplify expressions, solve equations, and find roots. Understanding factoring, including special cases, is essential for mastering algebraic concepts.

1. **Factoring Common Terms:** Identify common factors among the terms and factor them out.
2. **Factoring by Grouping:** Group terms together and factor out common factors from each group.
3. **Special Cases:**

   - **Difference of Squares:**

$$a^2 - b^2 = (a+b)(a-b)$$

- Perfect Square Trinomials:

$$a^2 + 2ab + b^2 = (a + b)^2$$
$$a^2 - 2ab + b^2 = (a - b)^2$$

Let's solve some examples:

1. Common Factor: $40n^3 - 8$

Identify the greatest common factor (GCF) of the terms:

$$40n^3 = 8 \times 5 \times n^3$$

$$8 = 2 \times 2 \times 2$$

$$GCF = 8$$

Factor out the GCF:

$$8(5n^3 - 1)$$

2. Factoring a Trinomial: $-54x^4 - 48x + 54x^3$

Group the terms and factor out the common factor from each group:

$$-6x(9x^3 + 8 - 9x^2)$$

3. Factoring a Difference of Squares: $16x^2 - 25$

Identify the difference of squares pattern and factor accordingly:

$$(4x - 5)(4x + 5)$$

4. Factoring a Perfect Square: $9n^2 - 12n + 4$

Identify the perfect square trinomial pattern and factor accordingly:

$$(3n - 2)^2$$

Linear Equation

A linear equation is an algebraic equation that represents a straight line when graphed on a coordinate plane. It consists of variables raised to the power of 1 (i.e., no exponents higher than 1) and constant coefficients.

The general form of a linear equation in one variable x is:

$$ax + b = 0$$

Where a and b are constants, and x is the variable.

Let's solve the linear equation:

$$-2x + 9 = 5$$

- **Isolate the variable term:** We want to isolate the term containing x on one side of the equation. To do this, we'll move the constant term to the other side. Subtract 9 from both sides:

$$-2x + 9 - 9 = 5 - 9$$

$$-2x = -4$$

- **Divide by the coefficient of the variable:** To solve for x, divide both sides by the coefficient of x, which is -2:

$$\frac{-2x}{-2} = \frac{-4}{-2}$$

$$x = 2$$

<u>Slop from Two Points</u>

The slope between two points on a Cartesian coordinate system is a measure of the steepness of the line connecting those points. It's calculated by finding the change in the y-coordinates divided by the change in the x-coordinates.

- The coordinates of the first point as $(x_1, y_1) = (2, -30)$.

- The coordinates of the second point as $(x_2, y_2) = (-5, 40)$.

The formula to calculate the slope (m) between two points:

$$\frac{y2 - y1}{x2 - x1}$$

$$= \frac{40 - (-30)}{-5 - 2} = \frac{70}{-7}$$

$$\text{Slope} = -10$$

Quadratic Equations

A quadratic equation is a polynomial equation of the second degree, meaning it can be written in the form:

$$ax^2 + bx + c = 0$$

where a, b, and c are constants, and x is the variable being solved for. The solutions to a quadratic equation are the values of x that make the equation true.

Now, let's solve the quadratic equation $11x^2 - 1 = 0$ and understand it step by step using quadratic formula.

1. **Identify the coefficients:**

   In the equation $11x^2 - 1 = 0$,

   $$a=11, b=0, \text{ and } c=-1.$$

2. **Apply the quadratic formula:**

   The quadratic formula states that for an equation $ax^2 + bx + c = 0$, the solutions for x are given by:

   $$x = \frac{-b \pm \sqrt{b^2 - 4ac}}{2a}$$

   Plugging in the values a=11, b=0, and c=−1 into the quadratic formula, we get:

   $$x = \frac{-0 \pm \sqrt{0 - 4(11)(-1)}}{2(11)}$$

3. Simplify inside the square root:

$$0^2 - 4(11)(-1) = 0 - (-44) = 44$$

4. Plug in the simplified values:

$$X = \frac{\pm \sqrt{44}}{22}$$

5. Simplify the square root:

Since 44 is not a perfect square, we can write it as $\sqrt[2]{11}$

$$X = \frac{\pm \sqrt[2]{11}}{22}$$

6. Simplify further if possible:

We can simplify $\sqrt[2]{11}$ to $\sqrt{11}$ by canceling out the common factor:

$$X = \frac{\pm \sqrt{11}}{11}$$

7. Final solution:

So, the solutions to the equation are:

$$X = \frac{\sqrt{11}}{11} \text{ and } x = \frac{-\sqrt{11}}{11}$$

or

$$(x = 0.302, \text{ and } x = -0.302)$$

These are the roots of the quadratic equation. They represent the points where the graph of the quadratic equation intersects the x-axis.

Let's solve another equation:

$$-4p^2 + 6p - 6 = 0$$

$$p = \frac{-b \pm \sqrt{b^2 - 4ac}}{2a}$$

where $a = -4$, $b = 6$, and $c = -6$.

Let's plug these values into the quadratic formula:

$$p = \frac{-6 \pm \sqrt{6^2 - 4(-4)(-6)}}{2(-4)}$$

First, let's simplify inside the square root:

$$6^2 - 4(-4)(-6)$$

$$= 36 - 96 = -60$$

So, we have:

$$p = \frac{-6 \pm \sqrt{-60}}{-8}$$

We can simplify the square root of −60 by factoring out −1:

$$\sqrt{-60}$$

$$= \sqrt{-1 \times 60}$$

$$= \sqrt{-1} \times \sqrt{60}$$

$$= i\sqrt{60}$$

So, we have:

$$p = \frac{-6 \pm i\sqrt{60}}{-8}$$

Simplify:

$$\sqrt{60} \text{ to } \sqrt{4 \times 15} = 2\sqrt{15}$$

$$p = \frac{-6 \pm i \times 2\sqrt{15}}{-8}$$

Now, divide both the numerator and denominator by −2 to simplify:

$$p = \frac{3 \pm i\sqrt{15}}{4}$$

So, the solutions to the equation are:

$$p = \frac{3 + i\sqrt{15}}{4} \quad \text{and} \quad p = \frac{3 - i\sqrt{15}}{4}$$

This equation -4p² + 6p - 6 = 0 has no real solutions.

When a quadratic equation has no real solutions, it means that the solutions are not real numbers, but rather complex numbers. In this case, the solutions involve the imaginary unit i because the discriminant ($b^2 - 4ac$) is negative, which results in taking the square root of a negative number when applying the quadratic formula.

In mathematics, such equations are said to have "no real roots" or "no real solutions." They are also sometimes referred to as having "complex roots" or "complex solutions." Complex numbers include a real part and an imaginary part, and they are often written in the form $a + bi$, where a and b are real numbers and i is the imaginary unit, defined as $i = \sqrt{-1}$.

Let's solve another equation:

$$12x^2 + 6x - 2 = 0$$

$$x = \frac{-b \pm \sqrt{b^2 - 4ac}}{2a}$$

where $a = 12$, $b = 6$, and $c = -2$.

Let's plug these values into the quadratic formula:

$$x = \frac{-6 \pm \sqrt{6^2 - 4(12)(-2)}}{2(12)}$$

First, let's simplify inside the square root:

$$6^2 - 4(12)(-2)$$

$$= 36 - (-96)$$

$$= 36 + 96$$

$$= 132$$

So, we have:

$$X = \frac{-6 \pm \sqrt{132}}{24}$$

Now, let's simplify the square root of 132:

$$X = \frac{-6 \pm \sqrt{4 \times 33}}{24}$$

$$X = \frac{-6 \pm 2\sqrt{33}}{24}$$

$$X = \frac{-6 \pm \sqrt{33}}{12}$$

So, the solutions to the equation are:

$$X = \frac{-6 + \sqrt{33}}{12} \text{ and } X = \frac{-6 - \sqrt{33}}{12}$$

or (x = 0.229, and x = -0.729)

Let's solve a quadratic equation where the right side is a number, instead of 0.

$$-8n^2 + 6n + 30 = 7$$

To solve the equation, we first need to bring all terms to one side to set the equation equal to zero:

$$-8n^2 + 6n + 30 - 7 = 0$$

Simplify:

$$-8n^2 + 6n + 23 = 0$$

Now, to solve for n, we can use the quadratic formula:

$$n = \frac{-b \pm \sqrt{b^2 - 4ac}}{2a}$$

where $a = -8$, $b = 6$, and $c = 23$.

Plugging these values into the formula, we get:

$$n = \frac{-6\pm\sqrt{6^2-4(-8)(23)}}{2(-8)}$$

$$n = \frac{-6\pm\sqrt{36+736}}{-16}$$

$$n = \frac{-6\pm\sqrt{772}}{-16}$$

Now, let's simplify the square root of 772. We can factor out 4:

$$\sqrt{772} = \sqrt{4 \times 193} = 2\sqrt{193}$$

So, our equation becomes:

$$n = \frac{-6\pm2\sqrt{193}}{-8}$$

So, the solutions to the equation are:

$$n = \frac{-3+\sqrt{193}}{-8} \text{ and } n = \frac{-3-\sqrt{193}}{-8}$$

$$or$$

$$(n = -1.362, \text{ and } n = 2.112)$$

Polynomials

A polynomial is an algebraic expression consisting of one or more terms, where each term is a constant, a variable, or a product of constants and variables raised to whole number exponents.

Examples of polynomials include:

- $(7v^2 + 2v^4) + (8v^2 + 4v^4)$
- $(2v + 4v^2 + 2) - (5v - 4v^4 - 6v^2)$
- $(7x - 5\,y)(2x - 6\,y)$
- $(6x^2 + 4xy + 6\,y^2)(8x^2 + 3xy + 3\,y^2)$
- $\dfrac{2x^3 + 8x^2 + 2x}{2x^2}$

Operations on Polynomials

Addition of Polynomials:

- To add polynomials, simply combine like terms.
- Like terms are terms that have the same variable(s) raised to the same power(s).
- For example, to add $3x^2 + 2x$ and $5x^2 - 7x$, group the like terms: $3x^2 + 5x^2$ and $2x - 7x$, then add each group separately.

Subtraction of Polynomials:

- To subtract polynomials, distribute the negative sign and then add.
- For example, to subtract $x^2 - 2x$ from $4x^2 + 3x$, distribute the negative sign to each term in the second polynomial: $-(x^2 - 2x)$, then add each term separately.

<u>Multiplication of Polynomials:</u>

- To multiply polynomials, use the distributive property and then combine like terms.

- For example, to multiply $(x + 2)(3x - 4)$, distribute each term in the first polynomial to each term in the second polynomial, then combine like terms.

<u>Division of Polynomials:</u>

- Division of polynomials involves dividing one polynomial by another. It can be done using long division or synthetic division.

Let's solve the expression:

$$(7x^2 - 7x) - (x - 2x^2)$$

Step 1: Distribute the Negative Sign:

Distribute the negative sign in the second polynomial:

$$(7x^2 - 7x) - x + 2x^2$$

Step 2: Combine Like Terms:

$$(7x^2 + 2x^2) + (- 7x - x)$$

Step 3: Perform addition and subtraction of coefficients:

$$9x^2 - 8x$$

Let's perform the multiplication of polynomials:

$$(5u + 2v)(8u^2 - uv - 3v^2)$$

We can distribute each term in the first polynomial $(5u+2v)$ to every term in the second polynomial $(8u2 - uv - 3v2)$.

1. Multiply $5u$ by each term in the second polynomial:

$$5u \cdot 8u^2 = 40u^3$$

$$5u \cdot (-uv) = -5u^2v$$

$$5u \cdot (-3v^2) = -15uv^2$$

2. Multiply $2v$ by each term in the second polynomial:

$$2v \cdot 8u^2 = 16u^2v$$
$$2v \cdot (-uv) = -2uv^2$$
$$2v \cdot (-3v^2) = -6v^3$$

Combine the like terms:

$$40u^3 - 5u^2v - 15uv^2 + 16u^2v - 2uv^2 - 6v^3$$

Combine the like terms involving u and v.

$$40u^3 + (16u^2v - 5u^2v) + (-15uv^2 - 2uv^2) - 6v^3$$
$$40u^3 + 11u^2v - 17uv^2 - 6v^3$$

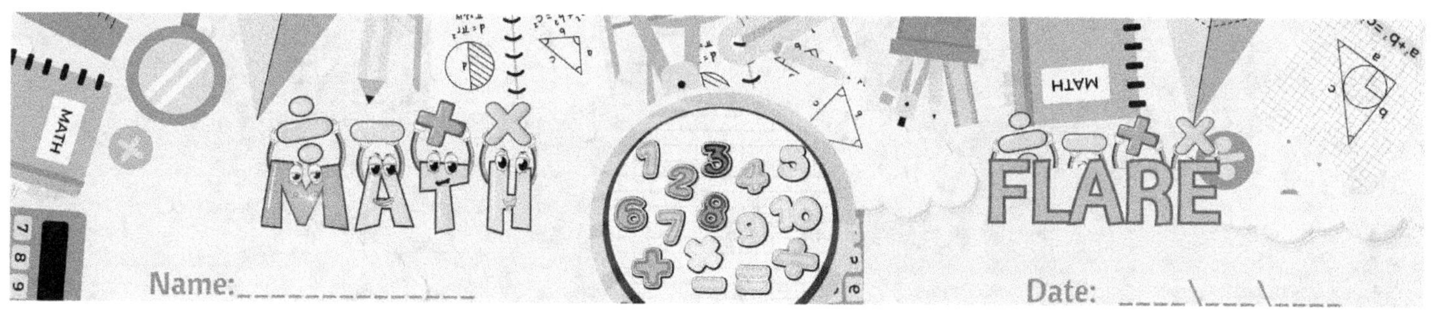

Equations: (One Side)

Solve the equations for the variable.

1. $19 - 18x = 1$

2. $19z + 3 = 307$

3. $4 + 16z = 196$

4. $-6x + -10 = -88$

5. $-6 + 5x = -6$

6. $12 - 2k = 24$

7. $m \times -2 = 6$

8. $z - -5 = 18$

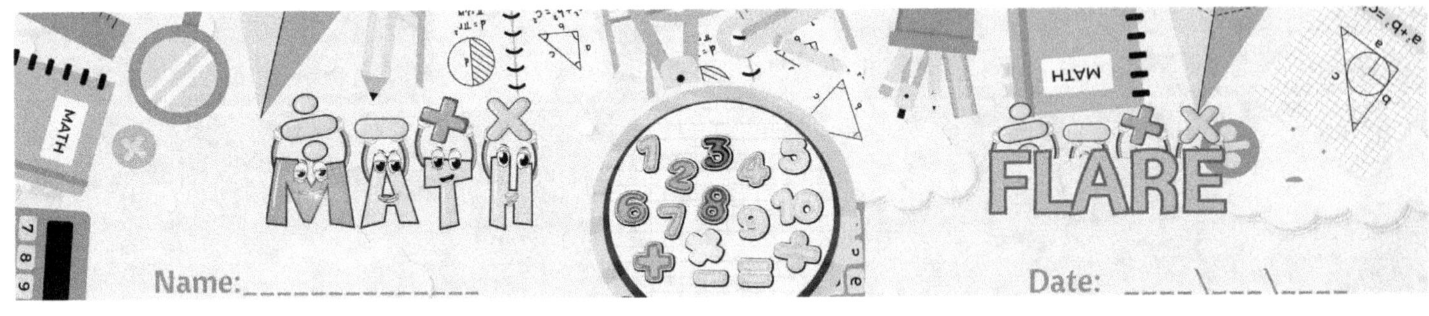

9. $10m - 17 = 183$

10. $11 - z = 8$

11. $x + 18 = 32$

12. $2 + 2z = 32$

13. $-9x + 20 = 110$

14. $y - -7 = 5$

15. $19 \times x = 114$

16. $k \div -3 = -9$

17. $y \div 6 = -8$

18. $m + -8 = -14$

19. $22 - 13z = 9$

20. $16 - k = 14$

21. $16 \times m = -160$

22. $-6 - 10z = 4$

23. $-9y + 17 = 62$

24. $m + -9 = -17$

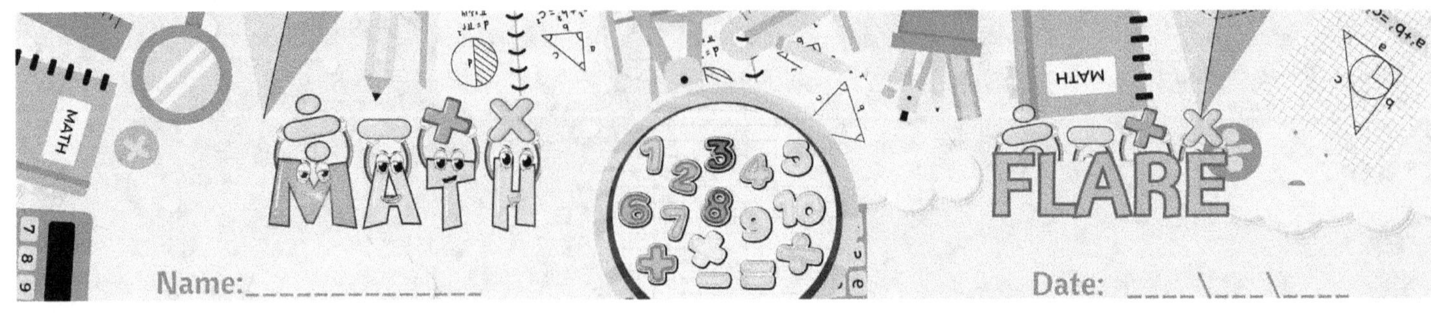

25. $18 - x = 14$

26. $y \div -4 = 0$

27. $0 - y = 8$

28. $56 - -8m = 8$

29. $z + 7 = 26$

30. $49 \div k = -7$

31. $m \div 3 = 20$

32. $13 - y = 20$

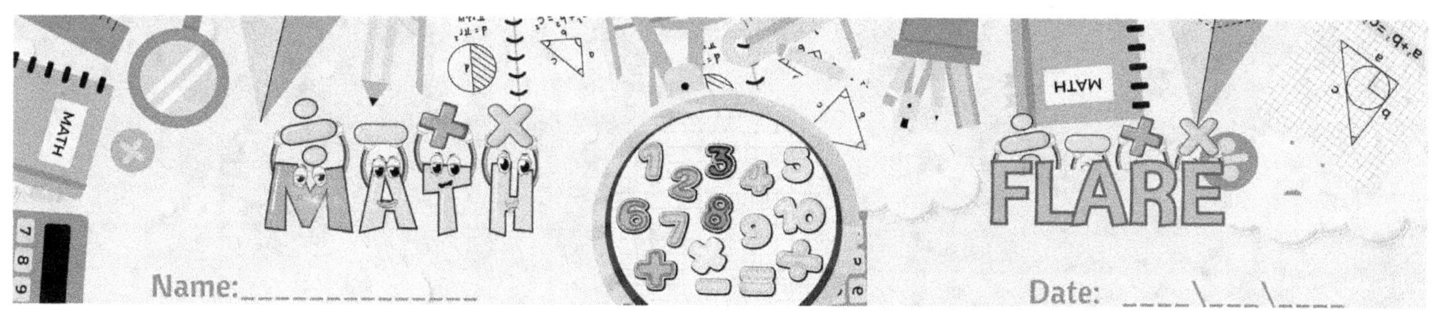

33. $17 - k = 12$

34. $15 - x = 4$

35. $10z + 4 = -76$

36. $6 - -7z = 132$

37. $8z - -7 = 159$

38. $12 + k = 22$

39. $17y - 0 = 238$

40. $z \div -5 = 9$

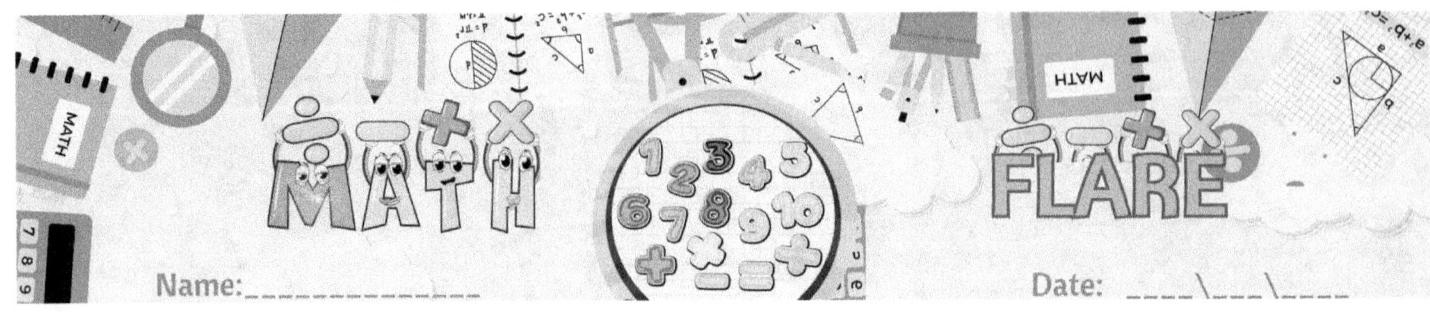

41. $154 \div k = 11$

42. $-6 + -2x = 4$

43. $k - 12 = 4$

44. $k + 3 = 3$

45. $17 + 15k = 62$

46. $m + -6 = 1$

47. $y - -7 = 3$

48. $k + 14 = 4$

Name:_________________   Date: ______________

49. $z - 0 = 1$

50. $40 - 8z = 8$

51. $12 - z = 2$

52. $z - 12 = 5$

53. $3m - 15 = 6$

54. $y + 6 = 8$

55. $x - {-3} = 11$

56. $-4 + x = 16$

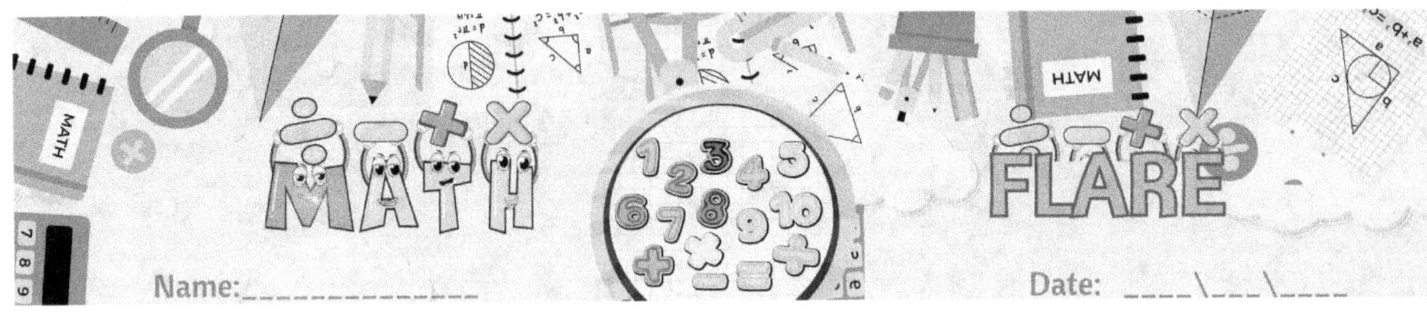

Equations: (Two Sides)

Solve for the variable.

1. $15 - m = 2m$

2. $99 - 7a = -3 + 10a$

3. $3 + 3s = 2s + 7$

4. $-6 - x = -4x$

5. $81 + m = -8m$

6. $10 + 4b + -4 = 0 + b$

7. $-2y = 24 + y$

8. $-5 + -5m = -41 + m$

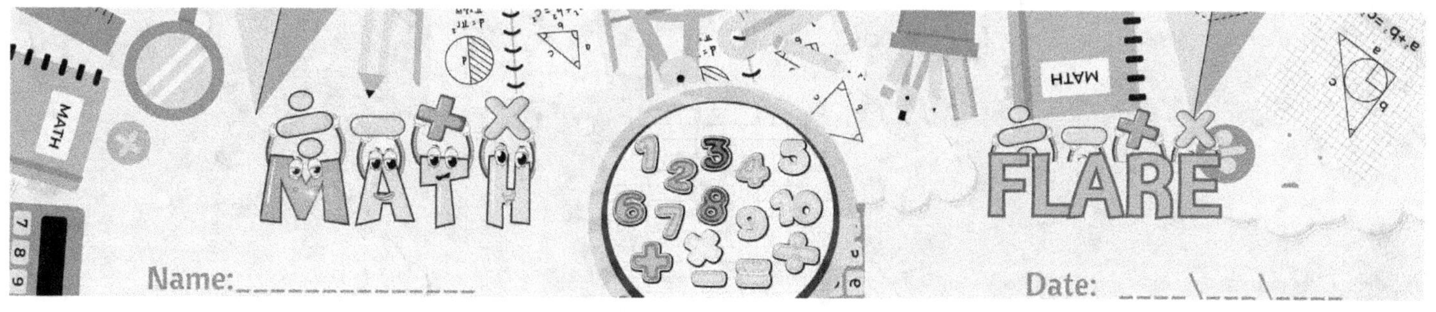

9. $-6 + 9y = -36 + 4y$

10. $-5 + 4a + 1 = 36 - a$

11. $9 + -6k + -5 = 51 + k + 2$

12. $18 + 2k = -2 + 7k$

13. $80 + x + 8 = 10 + -7x + -2$

14. $-5 + 9y = -145 + -5y$

15. $3b = -20 - b$

16. $-2z = -1 - z$

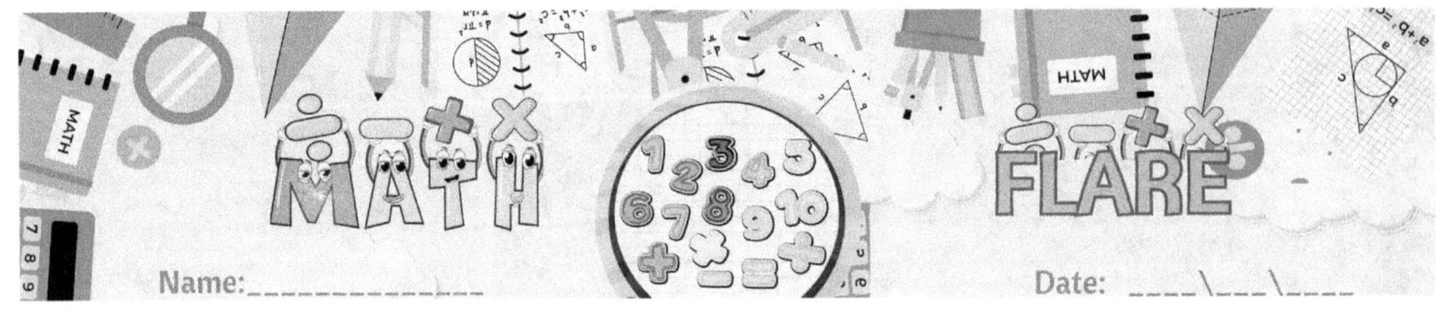

17. $5 + k = 3k + -9$

18. $52 - x = 4 + -9x$

19. $4 + -8b + 2 = 20 - b$

20. $2s = 5 + s$

21. $34 - a = 10 + 2a$

22. $-3 - x = 2x$

23. $85 + -10m = 10 + 5m$

24. $-9 + 7x = -105 - 5x$

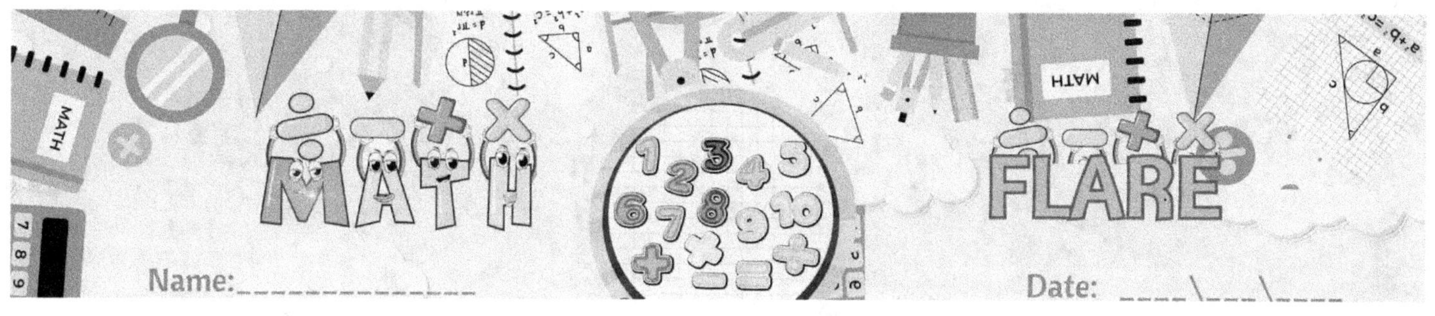

25. $2y = -8 + y$

26. $-8 + m = -7m$

27. $14 - s = -8s$

28. $-66 + m = -10m$

29. $58 + k = 9k + 2$

30. $-32 - -4k = 9k + 8$

31. $5 + 2x + -7 = -27 - x + -5$

32. $-113 - 2k = -5 + 10k$

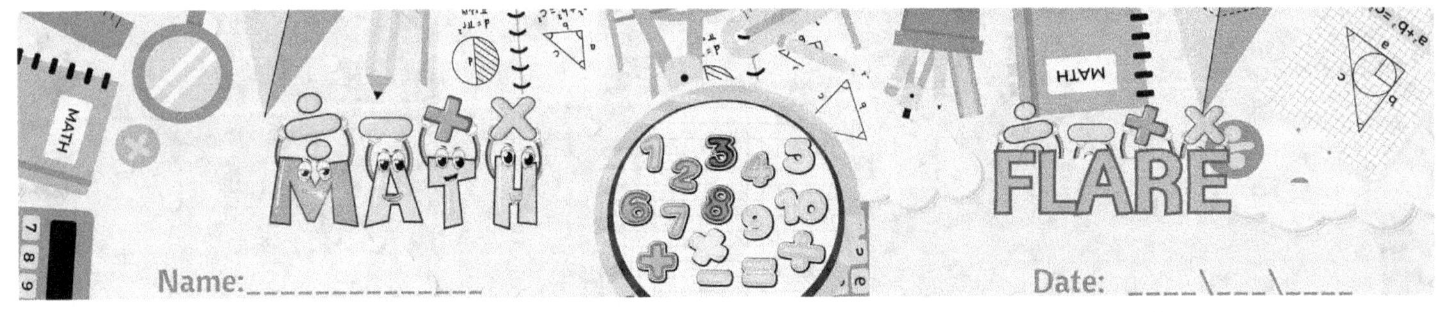

33. $1 + 8s + 10 = -39 + s + 15$

34. $4 + 5a + -3 = 42 + a + -5$

35. $18 + z + -6 = -2 + 4z + -1$

36. $-88 - 4a = 10a + 10$

37. $-90 - a = 9a$

38. $-7x + -84 = -4 + 1x$

39. $2k + 1 = 13 - k$

40. $-4m = -18 - m$

41. -5 - m = -6m

42. -8a = 70 - a

43. 1 + 1a = -62 - -8a

44. -56 - -5a = -1a + 4

45. 47 - s = 8s + -7

46. 8 + 9x + -3 = -12 - x + 7

47. -20 + k = 6k

48. -3 + 5k + -1 = -21 - k + -7

49. $-4 + 6b + 2 = 44 - b + 10$

50. $32 - -5k = -8 + -3k$

51. $1 + 10x = 15 - 4x$

52. $3 + -4k = -2 + k$

53. $4k + 10 = -12 + -7k$

54. $11 - z = -2z + 5$

55. $-8k = -70 - k$

56. $-2x = -6 + x$

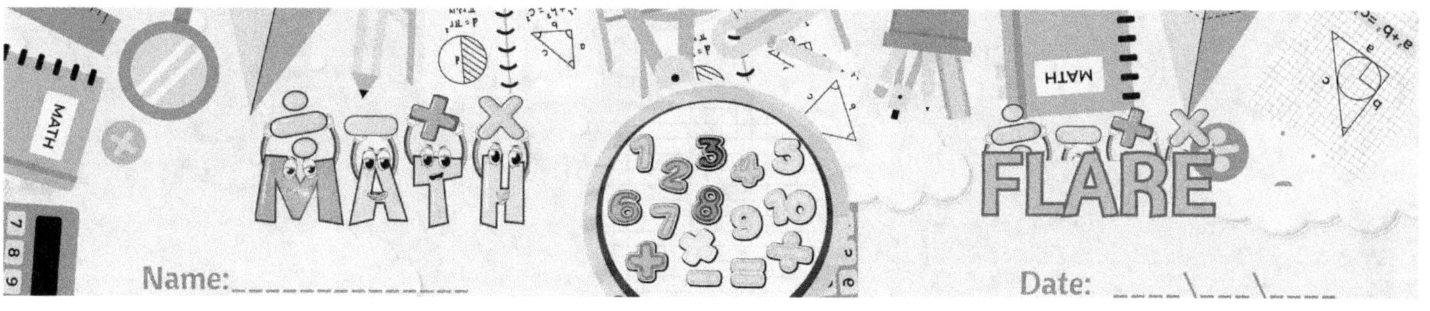

Solving One-Step Equations

Solve for the variable.

1. $17 = a + 9$

2. $45 = 9a$

3. $-b = -2$

4. $x + 2 = 3$

5. $-9 + x = -3$

6. $s + 8 = 16$

7. $4 = \dfrac{a}{2}$

8. $2 = a - 1$

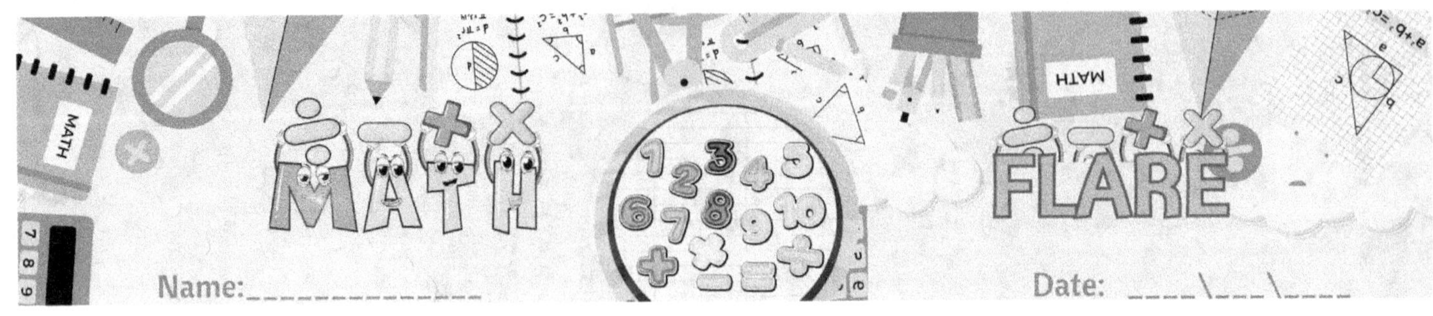

9. $-s = -6$

10. $8 = m + 2$

11. $\dfrac{a}{6} = 1$

12. $-4 = -7 + y$

13. $2 = \dfrac{y}{3}$

14. $\dfrac{z}{1} = 6$

15. $25 = 5m$

16. $54 = 9m$

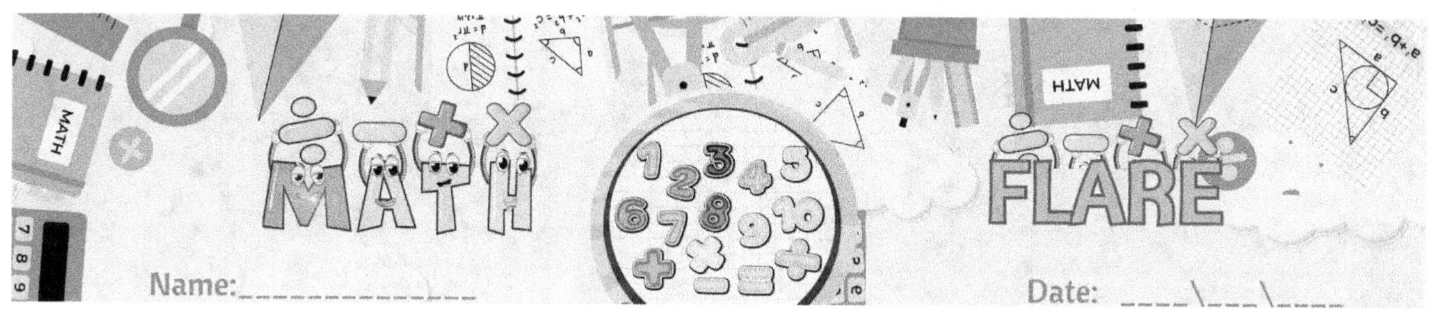

17. $x - 10 = -7$

18. $1 = \dfrac{m}{1}$

19. $2 = \dfrac{s}{2}$

20. $k + 1 = 5$

21. $16 = b + 6$

22. $-8 + a = 1$

23. $\dfrac{a}{1} = 10$

24. $-5 = b - 8$

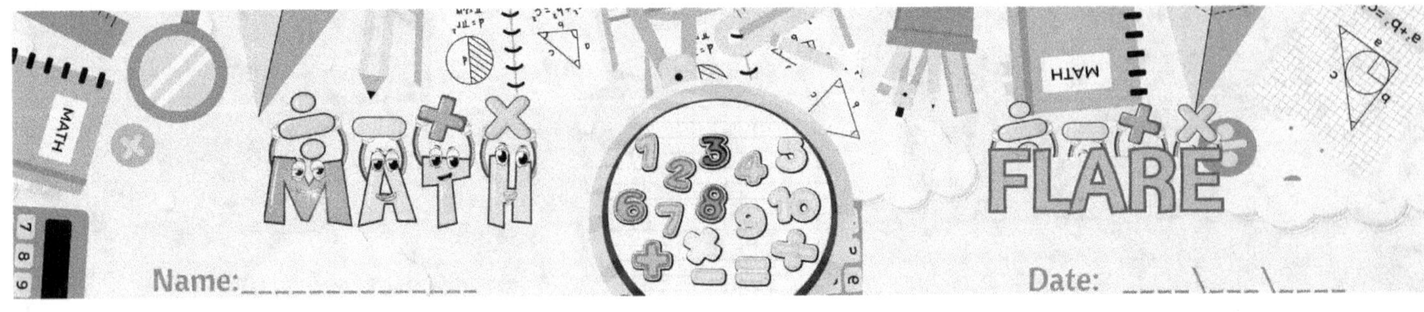

25. $5s = 40$

26. $6a = 48$

27. $8 = -2 + x$

28. $12 = s + 3$

29. $a + 4 = 12$

30. $z + 3 = 9$

31. $-5 + m = 2$

32. $-3 + x = 0$

33. $\dfrac{y}{8} = 1$

34. $-28 = -4m$

35. $m + 7 = 16$

36. $1 = \dfrac{m}{10}$

37. $4b = 28$

38. $-7s = -7$

39. $m - 2 = 7$

40. $-2 = s - 10$

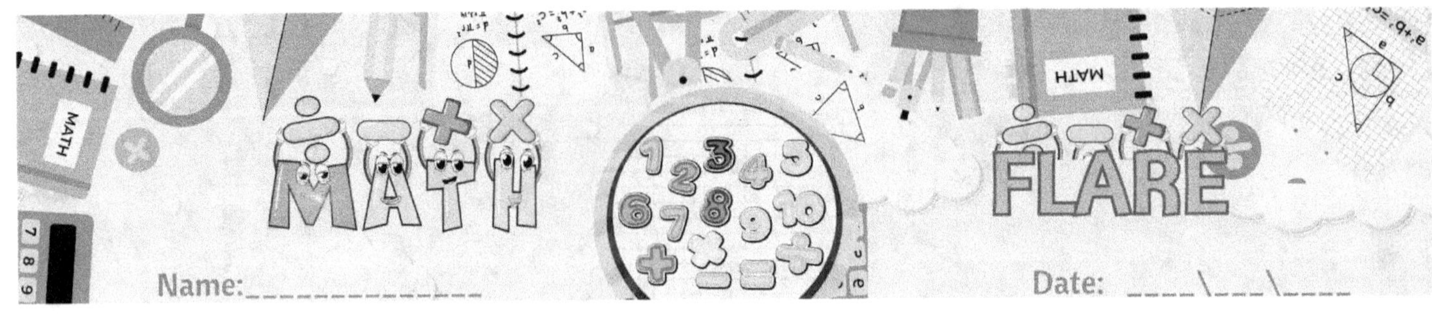

41. $2y = 10$

42. $-3z = -3$

43. $\dfrac{s}{1} = 4$

44. $-14 = -2z$

45. $5 = -5 + s$

46. $-6 + x = 0$

47. $7y = 35$

48. $12 = y + 8$

49. $z - 9 = 1$

50. $\dfrac{s}{1} = 8$

51. $-7y = -49$

52. $4b = 12$

53. $y - 7 = -3$

54. $-16 = -2z$

55. $k + 1 = 8$

56. $0 = k - 8$

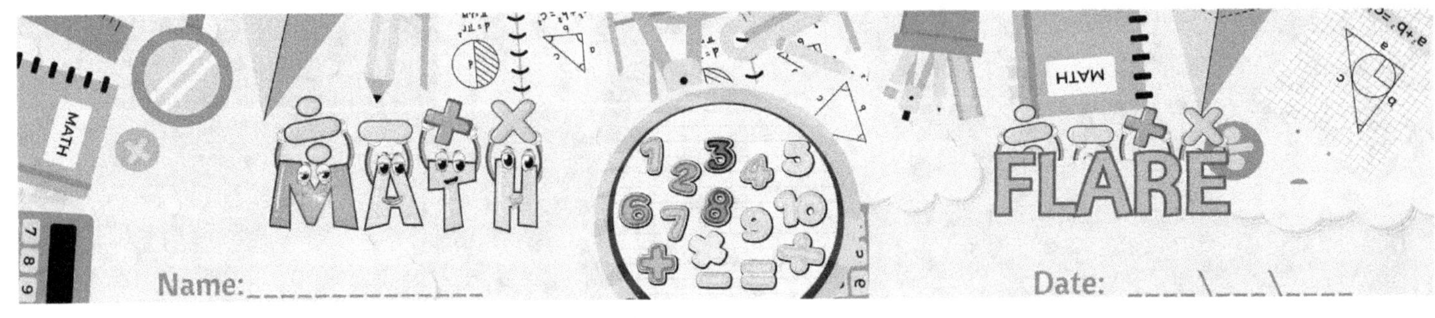

Solving Two-Step Equations

Solve for the variable.

1. $-13 = (7 - k) - 10$

2. $57 = 6s + 3$

3. $4b + 1 = 37$

4. $-2.4 = \dfrac{9 + s}{-8}$

5. $\dfrac{x}{-10} + 9 = 8$

6. $-39 = -7b - 4$

7. $96 = 8(2 + a)$

8. $3(4 + b) = 39$

9. $(-10 + m) - 5 = -7$

10. $5(9 + m) = 80$

11. $8k + 10 = 74$

12. $\dfrac{m}{-6} + 10 = 8.3$

13. $30 = 5(7 - x)$

14. $-9(-8 + x) = 54$

15. $\dfrac{6 + z}{-1} = -16$

16. $-10\,\dfrac{-x}{1} = 10$

17. $(2 + y) - 9 = -6$

18. $3.9 = \dfrac{y}{-8} + 4$

19. $-8(3 + s) = -80$

20. $-8 = (-3 + s) - 7$

21. $4 = (10 + z) - 10$

22. $-140 = -10(9 + x)$

23. $\dfrac{y}{1} + 6 = 7$

24. $3 = s - 2$

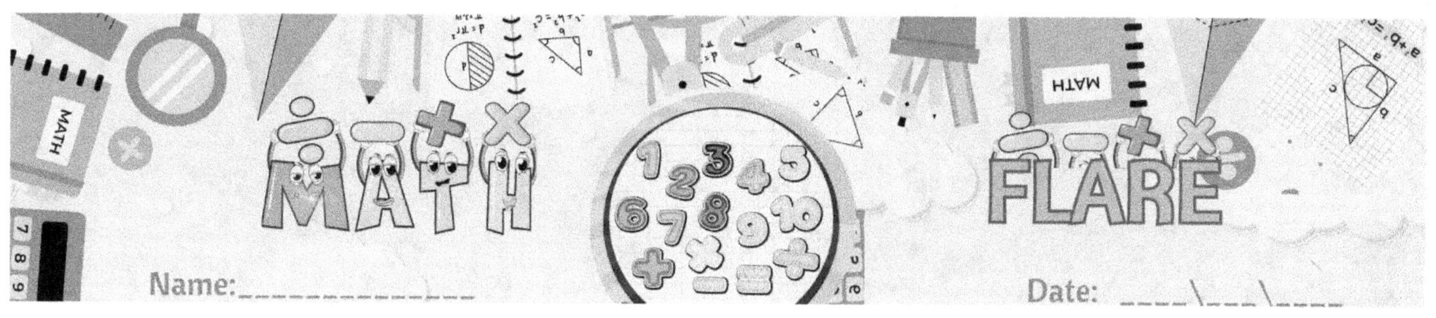

25. $7(-6 + a) = 14$

26. $-8 = \dfrac{y}{4} - 10$

27. $7 = 1(3 + z)$

28. $\dfrac{-8 + x}{2} = -2$

29. $4k + 2 = 30$

30. $10(5 + b) = 100$

31. $-5(6 + m) = -35$

32. $-27 = -10x - 7$

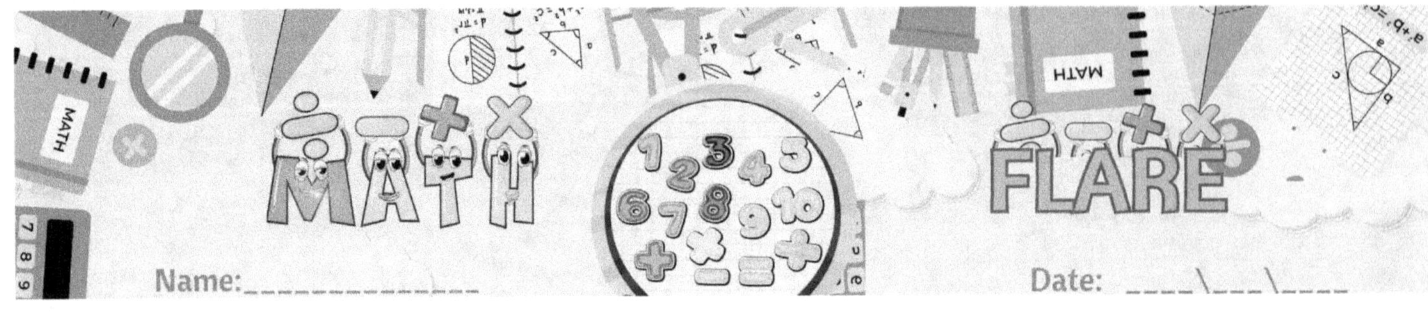

33. $-45 = -10k - 5$

34. $0 = \dfrac{a}{-1} + 6$

35. $-5z - 3 = -43$

36. $\dfrac{s}{-4} + 9 = 6.5$

37. $9 = \dfrac{x}{10} + 8$

38. $9.2 = \dfrac{a}{-10} + 10$

39. $66 = 6(8 + s)$

40. $-4 = 2(-3 + m)$

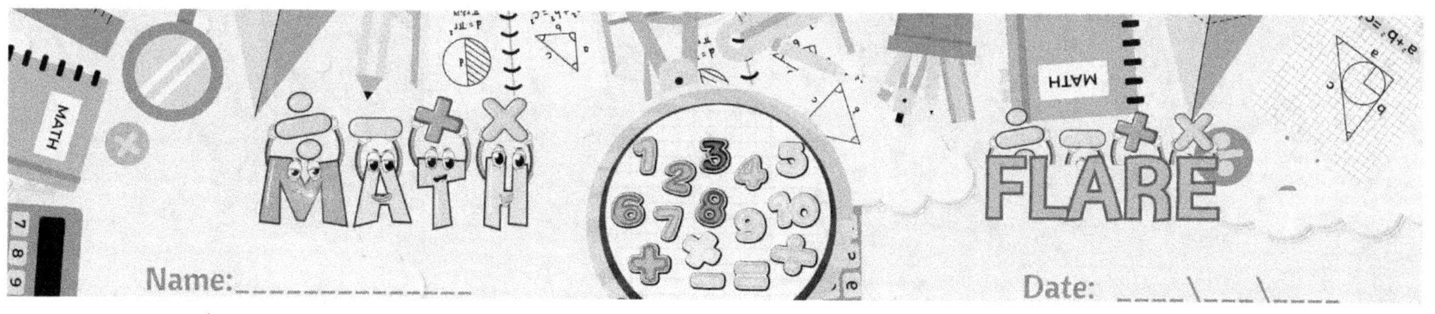

41. $8 + \dfrac{b}{4} = 10$

42. $40 = -4\,\dfrac{-k}{1}$

43. $66 = (7 + k)6$

44. $2k + 7 = 13$

45. $80 = 8(8 + m)$

46. $4m + 6 = 34$

47. $1(6 - z) = 0$

48. $56 = 4(8 + b)$

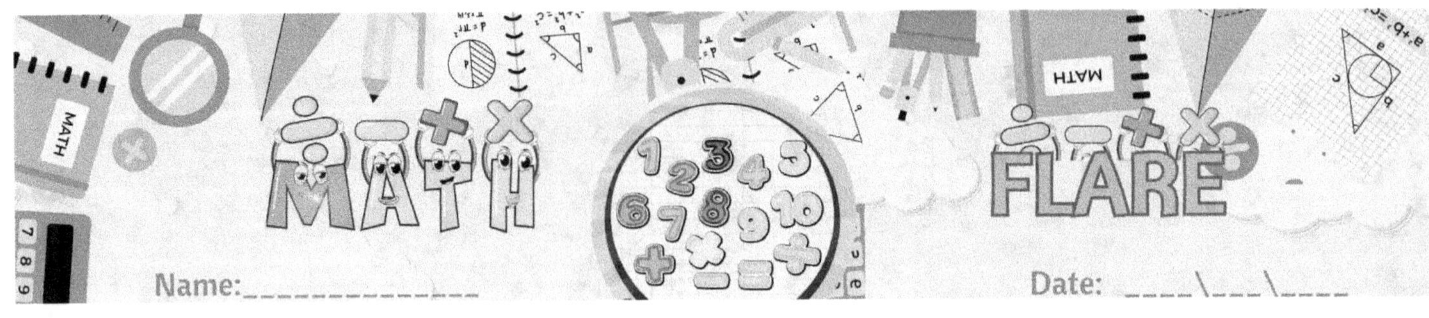

49. $5(2 - a) = 0$

50. $7 = (6 + m) - 1$

51. $-87 = -9z - 6$

52. $-12 = 4(5 - x)$

53. $1 - \dfrac{z}{5} = -1$

54. $(7 - z) - 3 = -1$

55. $\dfrac{m}{3} + 1 = 3$

56. $-29 = -4s - 1$

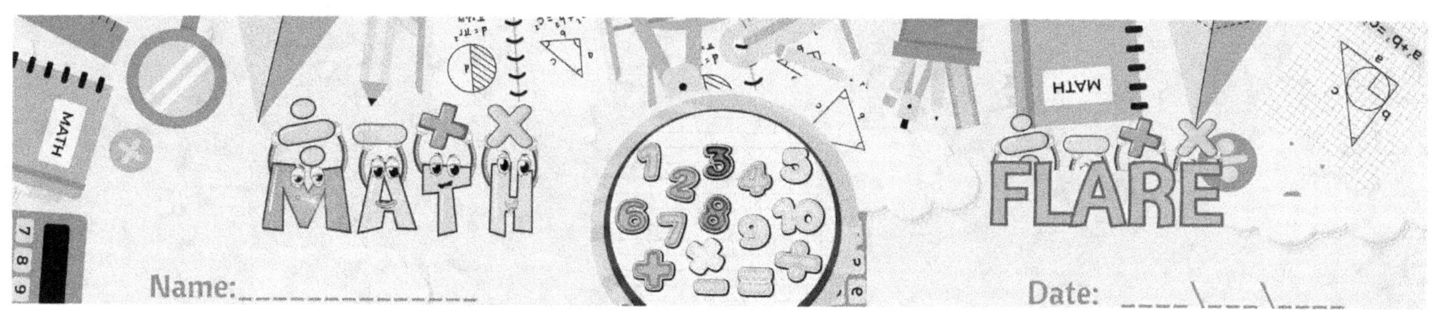

Solving Multi-Step Equations
Solve for the variable.

1. $-47 = -8z + 2 + z$

2. $5 + 5b - 4b = 10$

3. $6x + 3 + x = 73$

4. $1 - z + 1 = -8$

5. $59 = 5 + y + 5y$

6. $6 + 8k + 5k = 45$

7. $5x + 9x = 56$

8. $-14 = -8b - 1 - 5$

9. $m - 6 + 6m = 36$

10. $-15 = -1 - 7z - 7$

11. $21 = 4y - y$

12. $-5z - 3 - z = -33$

13. $-32 = -8 - x - 3x$

14. $-10x - 8 - 7 = -65$

15. $73 = 9 - y + 9y$

16. $-2a - a = -12$

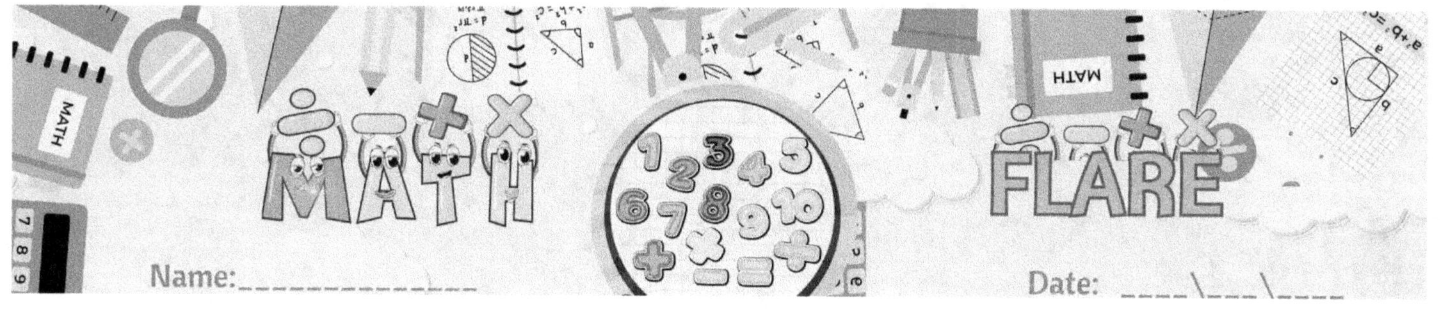

17. $-1 - z - 3z = -41$

18. $4 + a - 7a = -14$

19. $5 + 5m + 10m = 140$

20. $-70 = 5 - 8k + 5$

21. $-35 = -10b + 2 + 3$

22. $-6 = -10z + 5 - z$

23. $-19 = k - 9 - 3k$

24. $-30 = -5x - x$

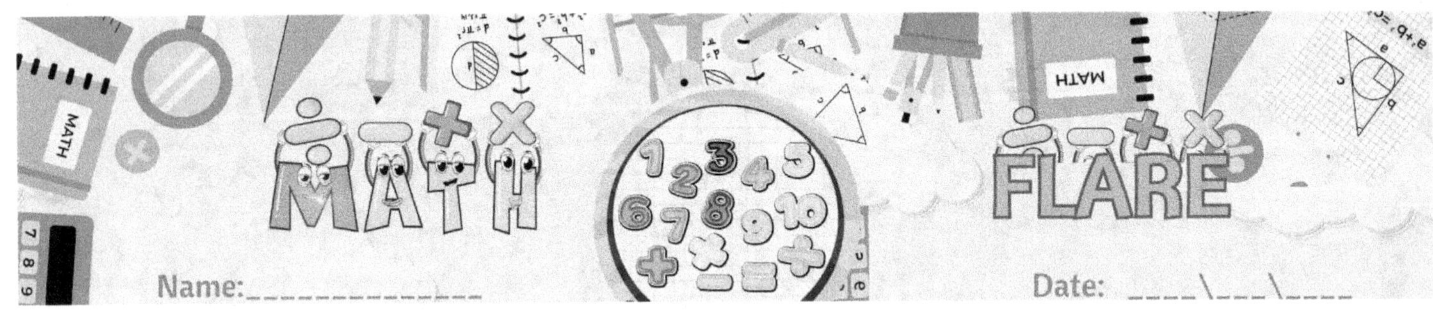

25. $-10s + 2 - 5 = -53$

26. $9x - 4 + x = 76$

27. $-8k - 1 - 4 = -61$

28. $10 - k - 8k = -26$

29. $-5 = -y + 10 - 6$

30. $-1 = 9 + 2x - 4x$

31. $-56 = -7 - 6m + 5$

32. $-9k + 9 + k = 1$

Name:_________________

Date: ____________

33. $-6z - z = -7$

34. $11 = k - 9 + k$

35. $-8z + 4z = -40$

36. $-4 + b - 4 = -1$

37. $3a + 9a = 108$

38. $-x + 2 + 10x = 11$

39. $3z - z = 2$

40. $-5 = 7 + a - 3a$

41. $-39 = k - 3 - 10k$

42. $43 = -7 + 8m - 6$

43. $81 = 5 + 10z + 9z$

44. $3 = -a + 3 + a$

45. $y - y = 0$

46. $49 = 1 + b + 7b$

47. $46 = 6 + 2m + 3m$

48. $-5m + 5 + m = -31$

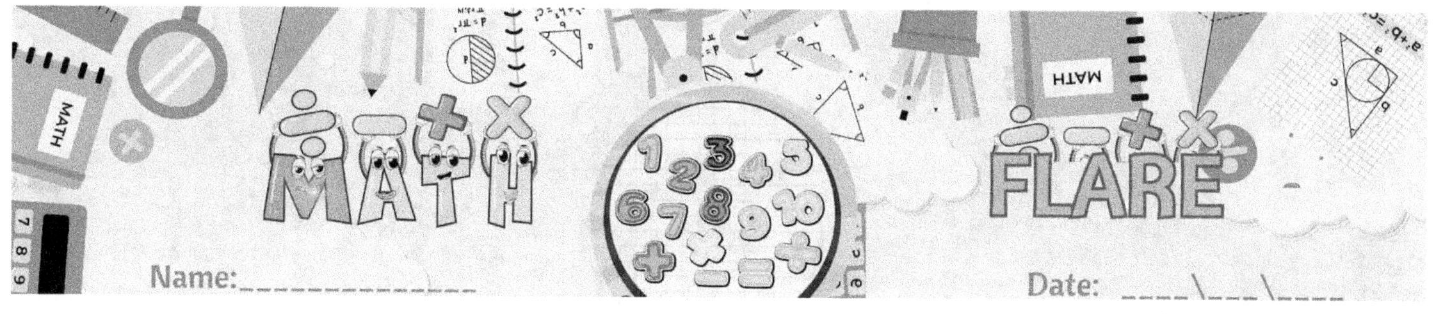

49. $-50 = -8 - b - 6b$

50. $-10 - 3y + 9y = -4$

51. $-7m - 10 - m = -66$

52. $-y + 8 - y = 4$

53. $112 = 8z + 8z$

54. $-1 - 4z - 9 = -42$

55. $-8 - m + 6m = -3$

56. $-5 = -3a - 2a$

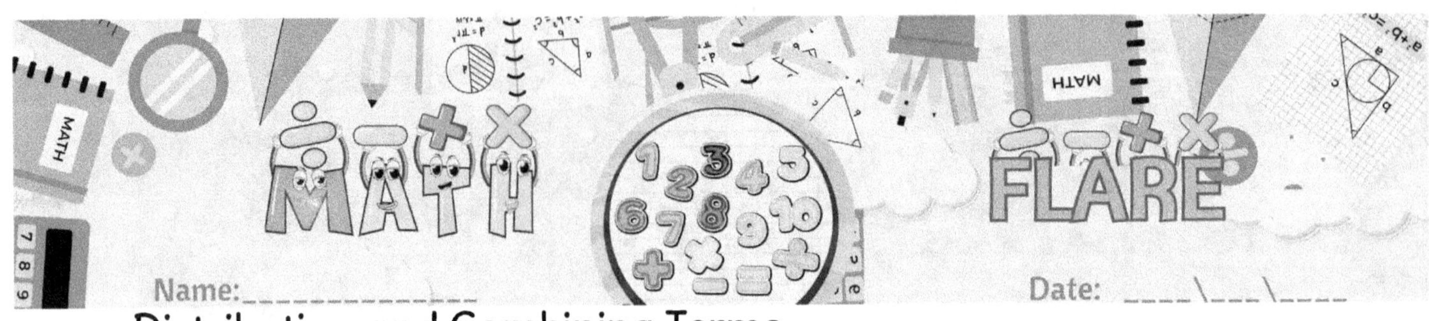

Distributing and Combining Terms

1. -3x + 1 + x - 3

2. 8b + 10b

3. x - 4 + 2

4. -2n + 3n

5. -4x + x

6. 6r + 2r

7. -6a - 2a

8. r - 8 + 6r + 8

9. -7x + 5x

10. 3n + 8 - 10 + 4n

Name:_________________

Date: _____________

11. -(10 p - 4)

16. -4(4 p + 4)

12. 10(4 + 9m)

17. 4(5x + 2)

13. -5(2a + 7)

18. 7(1 - 8x)

14. -9(9b + 4)

19. -5(1 + 6x)

15. 7(2n + 7)

20.5(-9b - 7)

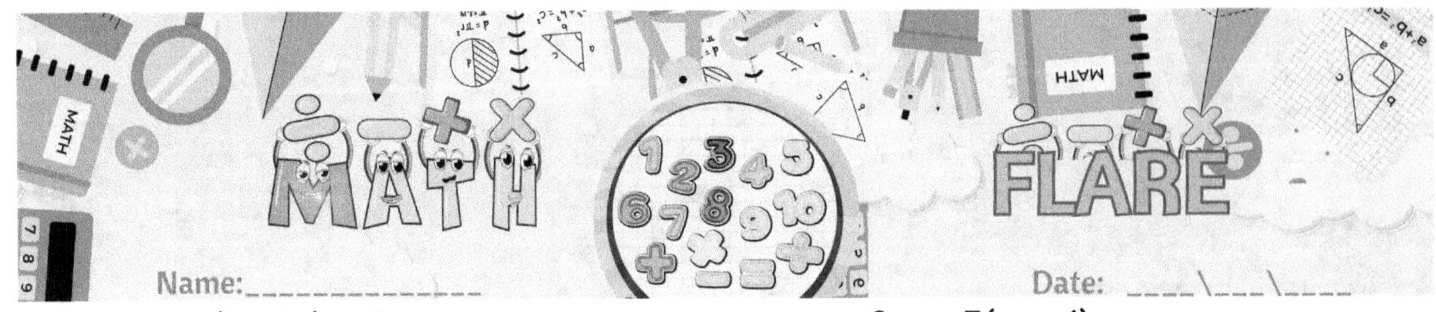

Name:________________   Date: ____________

21. -7(1 - 4a) + 6

22. -9x - 2(-2 + 9x)

23. -1 + 10(2 - 4a)

24. 2(k - 1) + 2

25. -4(-7 + 6m) + 7

26. -9m + 3(m + 1)

27. 3 - 6(5m - 9)

28. 10(6x + 3) - 9

29. 9(1 - 5x) + 5x

30. 6(5k - 9) + 10k

31. 10(x - 8) + 8(8x + 10)

32. 10(x + 2) + 8(x - 5)

33. -2(1 - 5 p) - 8(p + 7)

34. -10(4 - 2v) - 9(6v - 9)

35. 6(7 - r) - 9(r - 4)

36. -7(1 + 2m) - 5(6 + 6m)

37. -4(10 - m) - 10(7m + 7)

38. 8(5 - 10x) - 2(x + 7)

39. -9(x - 6) - 6(-1 - 5x)

40. -3(5r - 9) + 9(8r - 1)

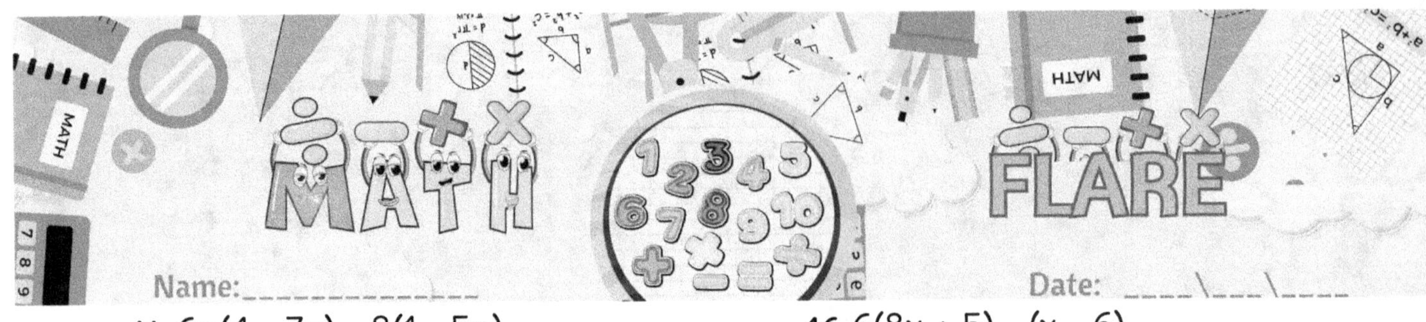

41. 6n(4 - 7n) - 8(1 - 5n)

42. -k(7k + 5) - 8k(1 - 5k)

43. -2n(1 - n) - 5(3n + 4)

44. 5r(4 + 3r) + 6(1 - 2r)

45. -6(-x - 6) + 2(2 + 7x)

46. 6(8x + 5) - (x - 6)

47. -6(6v - 5) + 7v(v + 8)

48. 4m(m - 8) - 2(m + 7)

49. -7 p(7 p - 6) - 4(p + 3)

50. -4(n + 5) + 4(n + 2)

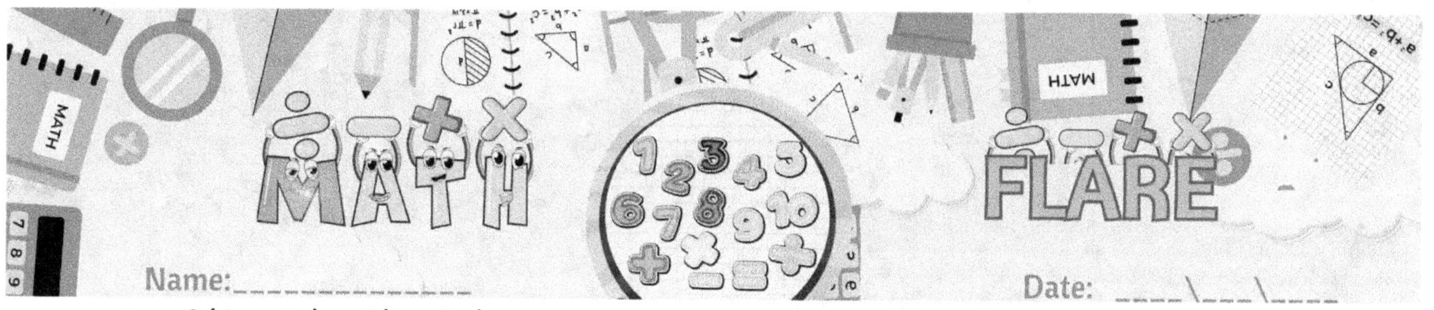

51. -8(4 + 5x) - 7(1 - 8x)

52. -3(3 - m) - 4(-6m - 2)

53. -6(-2k + 5) - 3(6k - 1)

54. -3(-8n + 1) - 2(1 - 6n)

55. -2(p - 8) - 4(1 + 5 p)

56. -7(6k - 4) - 3(5 - 4k)

57. -5(p + 2) - 6(1 - 8 p)

58. -5(6 + 7x) - 8(8x - 1)

59. -(8x + 1) - 7(1 - 4x)

60. -2(1 + 8x) - 2(x - 3)

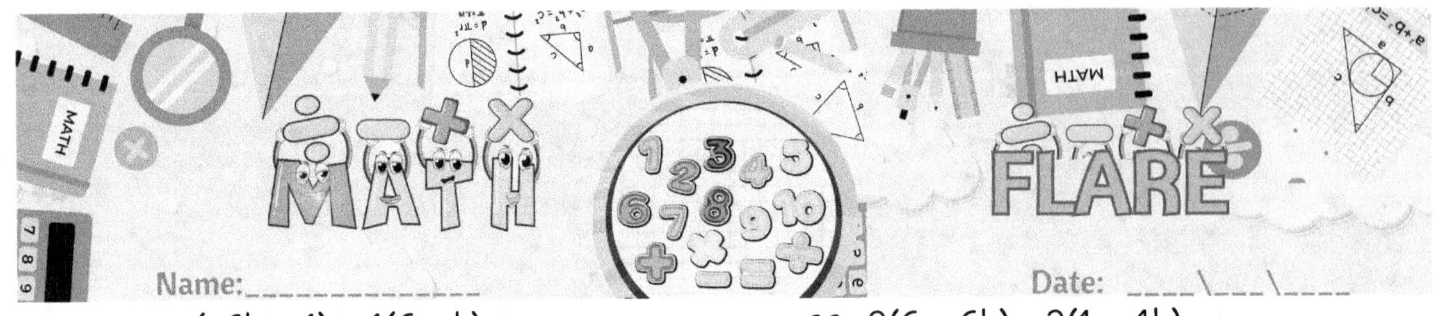

61. $-(-6k - 4) - 4(6 + k)$

66. $-2(6 + 6b) - 2(1 + 4b)$

62. $-5(1 + 7p) - 3(2p - 1)$

67. $-2(8x + 5) - 2(-4 + 2x)$

63. $-7(-7x - 5) - 8(8x + 5)$

68. $-3(1 + x) - (1 + x)$

64. $-7(-2n + 4) - (-6n - 7)$

69. $-2(-4a - 4) - 4(-a - 2)$

65. $-4(n - 6) - 2(1 + 6n)$

70. $-3(3n - 1) - 6(n + 7)$

Factoring with Special Cases

1. $40n^3 - 8$

2. $24b^2 + 8$

3. $40r^5 - 70r^3$

4. $-18x^6 - 12x$

5. $-5 - 45p$

6. $35m^3 - 14$

7. $-40 - 35b^3$

8. $25n + 10$

9. $-54n^2 + 9n$

10. $64x - 72x^2$

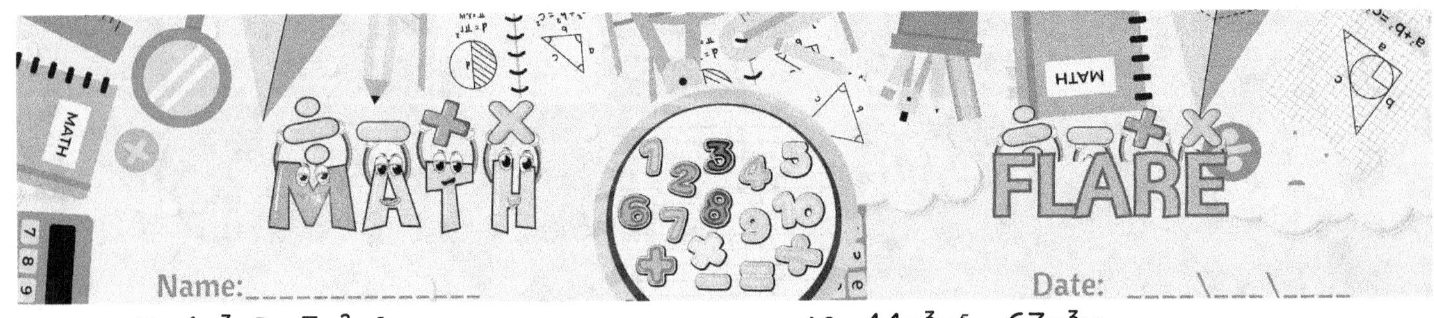

11. $4x^3y^7 - 3x^2y^5$

16. $-14x^3y^5 - 63x^3y$

12. $2a^5b^6 - 3a^7b^7$

17. $6x^4y^2 - x^2y$

13. $3x + 3x^2y$

18. $-48nm^2 - 56n$

14. $18ab^{14} + 12a^3b^9$

19. $-28xy^5 + 21x^2$

15. $-56x^2y^2 + 49x^2$

20. $20xy - 36x^2$

21. $12b - 12b^3 + 18b^4$

26. $-40n^5 + 30n^3 + 40n^2$

22. $16b^4 + 24b^2 + 64b$

27. $-20 + 30x + 25x^2$

23. $40k^4 - 50k^3 + 90k^2$

28. $7n^4 + 9n^3 + 2n$

24. $-54x^4 - 48x + 54x^3$

29. $6n^7 - 30n^5 + 60n^4$

25. $-18x^3 - 6x^2 - 30x$

30. $8x^4 - 8x^3 + 8x^2$

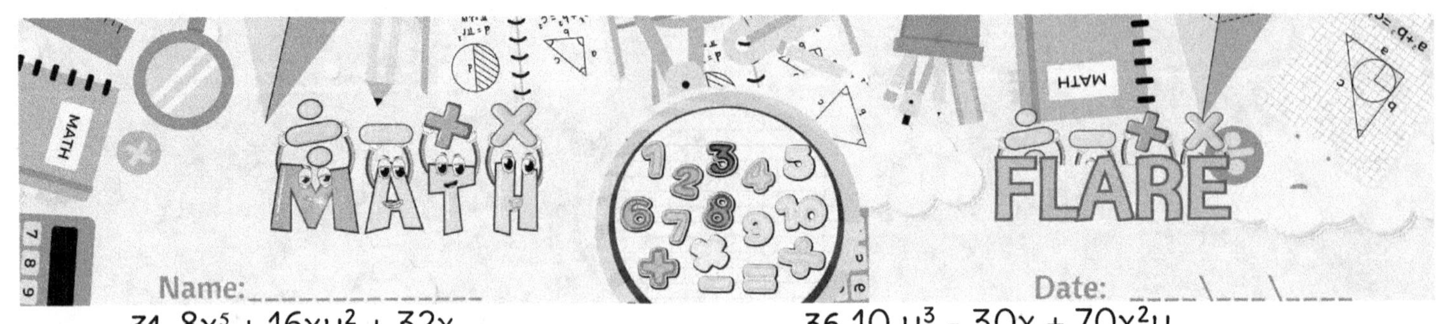

31. $8x^5 + 16xy^2 + 32x$

32. $24 y^3 + 64 yx + 24 y$

33. $-36n^4 + 63nm^2 + 81n^2$

34. $3x^3 + 3x^2y + 5x$

35. $-12xy - 8x^2 + 32x$

36. $10 y^3 - 30x + 70x^2y$

37. $6n^4m^4 - 36n^6m + 48n^3$

38. $-14 y + 35 + 28x$

39. $6xy - 48 y - 24$

40. $63a^4b^3 + 49a^2b^4 + 63a^2b^3$

Factoring: Difference of two Square

41) $9b^2 - 1$

42) $4b^2 - 1$

43) $25b^2 - 1$

44) $16n^2 - 9$

45) $x^2 - 16$

46) $n^2 - 4$

47) $16x^2 - 25$

48) $25r^2 - 16$

49) $25x^2 - 4$

50) $x^2 - 1$

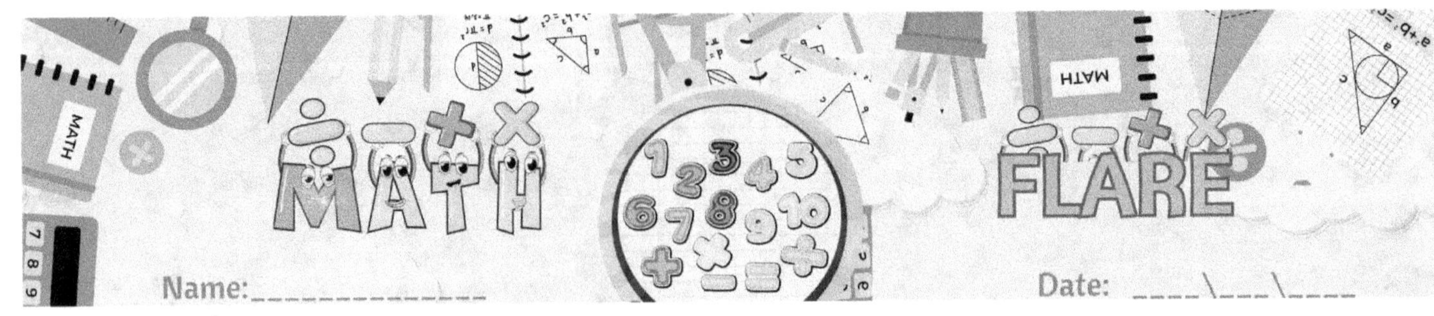

Name:_______________   Date: _______________

Factoring: Perfect Square

51) $9n^2 - 12n + 4$

52) $x^2 - 2x + 1$

53) $x^2 + 2x + 1$

54) $9x^2 - 30x + 25$

55) $9k^2 + 6k + 1$

56) $25p^2 + 30p + 9$

57) $16n^2 - 24n + 9$

58) $16m^2 + 40m + 25$

59) $x^2 + 8x + 16$

60) $k^2 + 6k + 9$

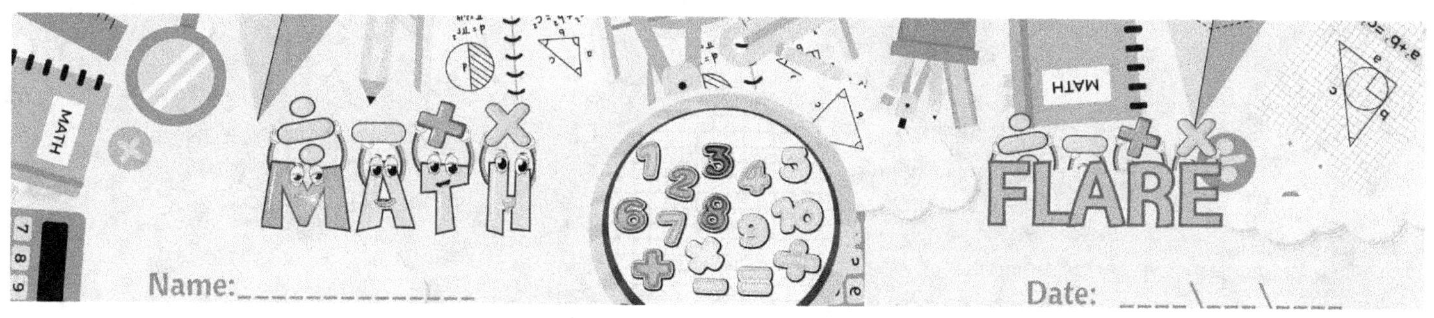

Standard Linear Equations

1. $-7x + 7 = -49$

2. $8x + 8 = -72$

3. $-9x + 4 = 76$

4. $1x + 9 = 12$

5. $9x + 0 = -18$

6. $3x + -8 = -8$

7. $-2x + 10 = 0$

8. $-7x + 0 = 7$

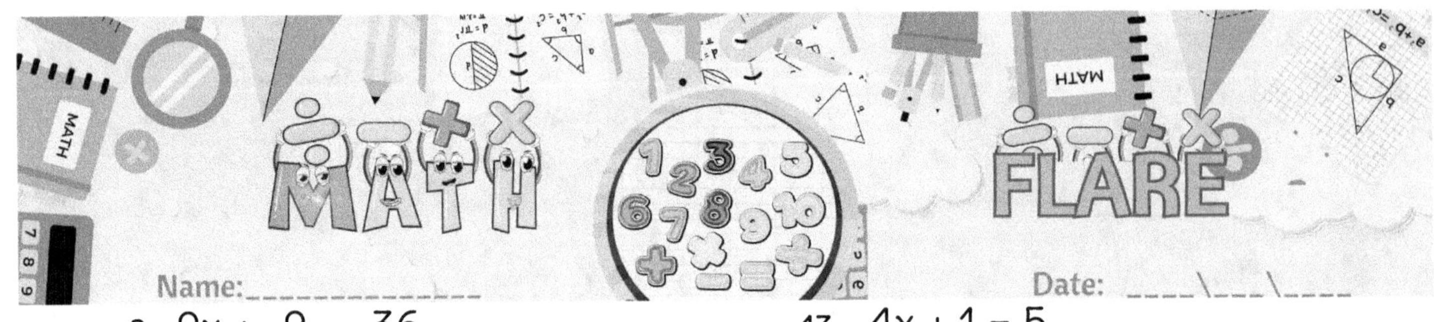

9. 9x + -9 = -36

13. -4x + 1 = 5

10. 4x + 2 = 6

14. 5x + 1 = -24

11. -2x + 6 = 20

15. 9x + -1 = 71

12. 10x + 4 = -56

16. 8x + -5 = -85

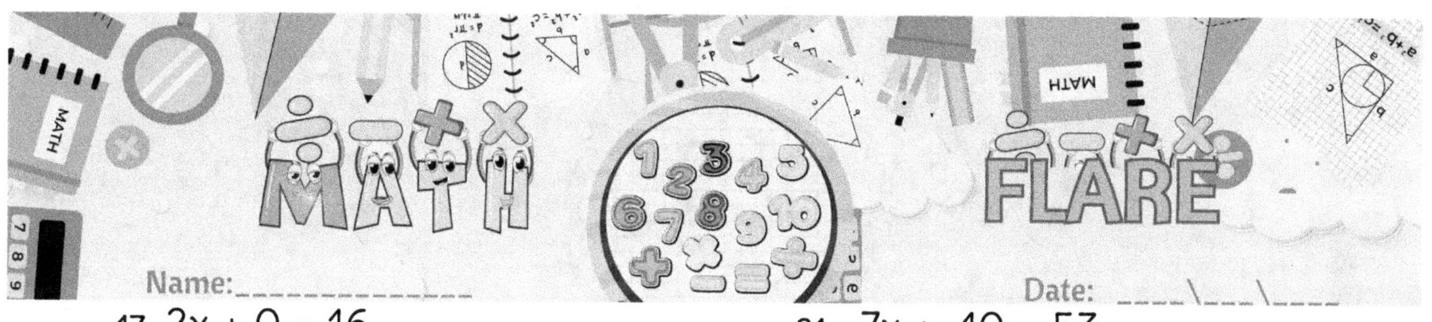

17. $2x + 0 = 16$

21. $-7x + -10 = 53$

18. $1x + -9 = -12$

22. $-1x + -1 = -2$

19. $-9x + 2 = -25$

23. $7x + 9 = -40$

20. $6x + 4 = 64$

24. $-10x + -9 = -9$

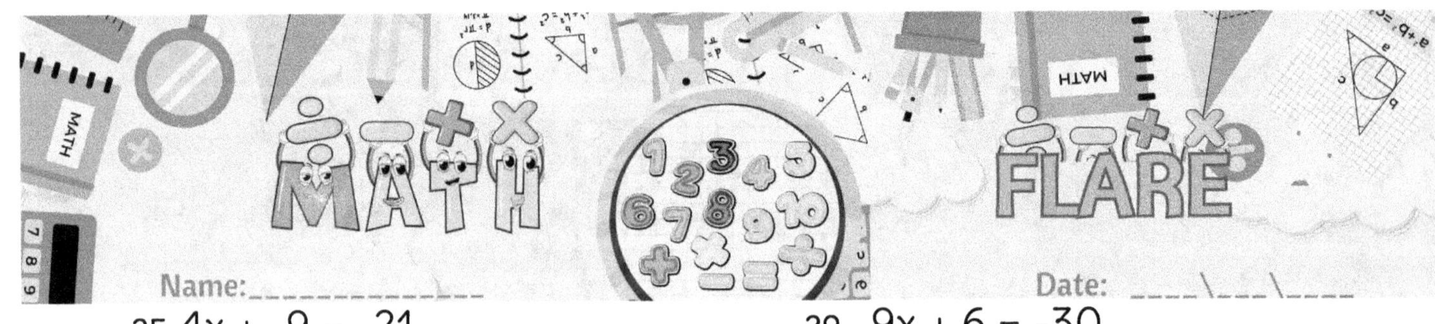

25. 4x + -9 = -21

29. -9x + 6 = -30

26. 3x + -9 = -33

30. 4x + -5 = -33

27. 10x + -2 = -92

31. -3x + 10 = -14

28. -6x + 1 = 13

32. 9x + -2 = -20

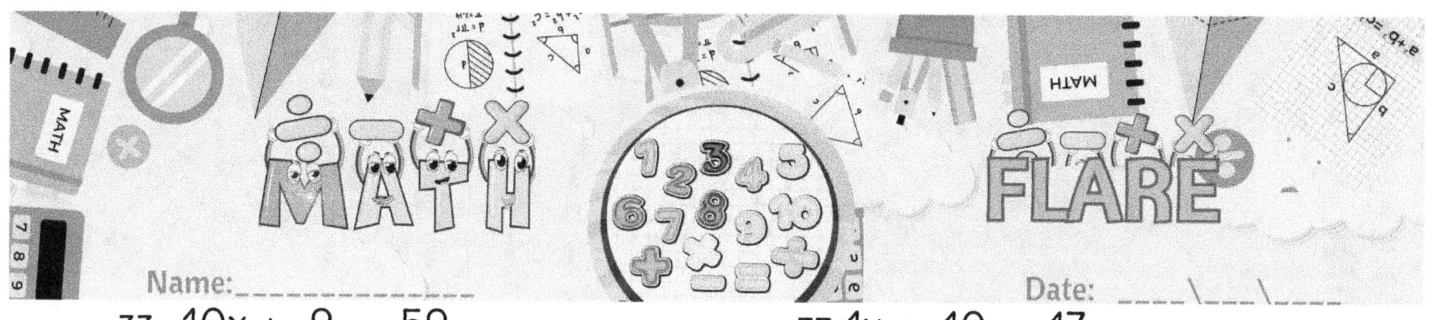

33. -10x + -9 = -59

37. 1x + -10 = -17

34. 8x + 10 = -70

38. 9x + 4 = -32

35. 9x + 9 = 54

39. 5x + -2 = 43

36. -7x + 9 = -47

40. 1x + -2 = -6

Find Slope from Two Points

1. (-8, -41) and (9, 61)

2. (-7, 39) and (-7, 39)

3. (5, -31) and (0, -6)

4. (1, 11) and (-3, -5)

5. (-10, -100) and (4, 26)

6. (-4, -28) and (10, 42)

7. (-2, -12) and (5, 51)

8. (5, -11) and (-10, 49)

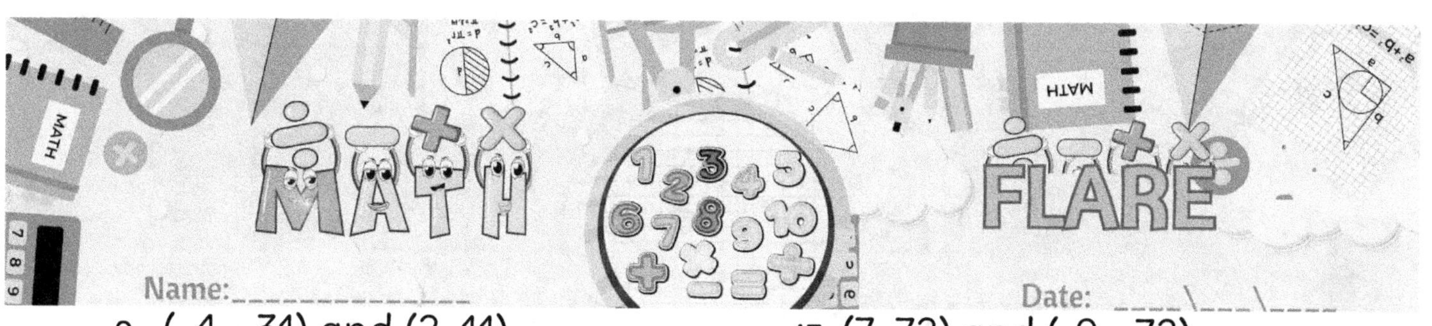

9. (-4, -31) and (2, 11)

13. (7, 72) and (-9, -72)

10. (2, -2) and (1, 1)

14. (5, -25) and (-5, 25)

11. (4, -29) and (-1, -4)

15. (4, -8) and (-10, 48)

12. (3, -10) and (-2, 5)

16. (2, -9) and (-9, 2)

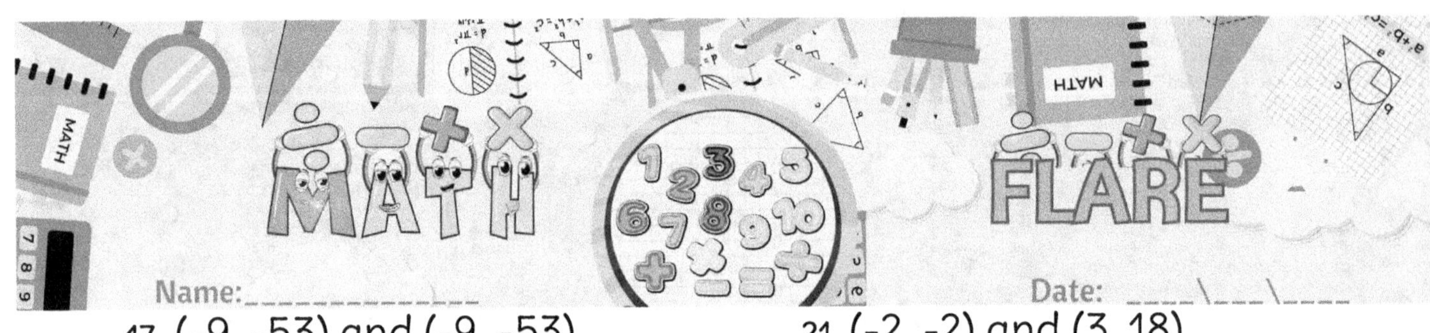

17. (-9, -53) and (-9, -53)

21. (-2, -2) and (3, 18)

18. (-4, 12) and (-2, 10)

22. (-7, 49) and (2, -5)

19. (10, 50) and (-3, -28)

23. (2, -8) and (-2, 24)

20. (9, 80) and (-2, -19)

24. (-6, -38) and (4, 12)

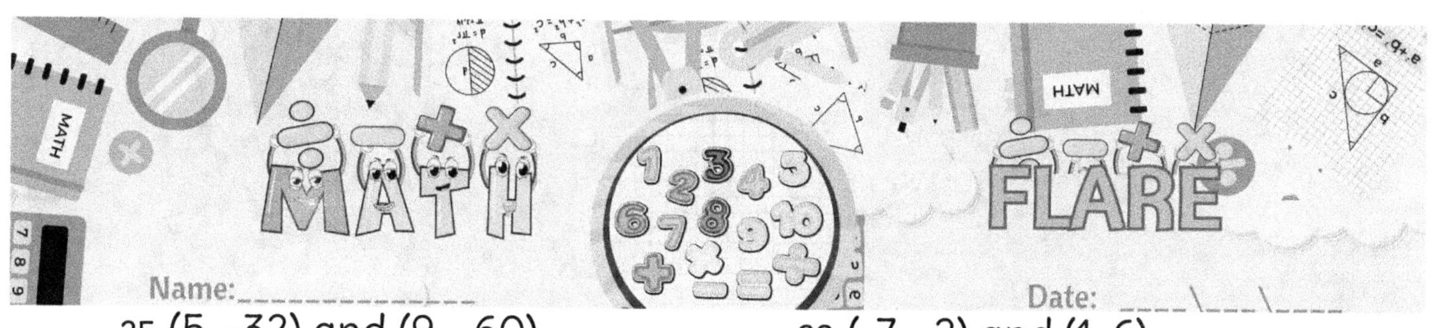

25. (5, -32) and (9, -60)

29. (-7, -2) and (1, 6)

26. (-10, 45) and (3, -7)

30. (-3, -10) and (-5, -20)

27. (7, -29) and (9, -37)

28. (5, -41) and (-3, 39)

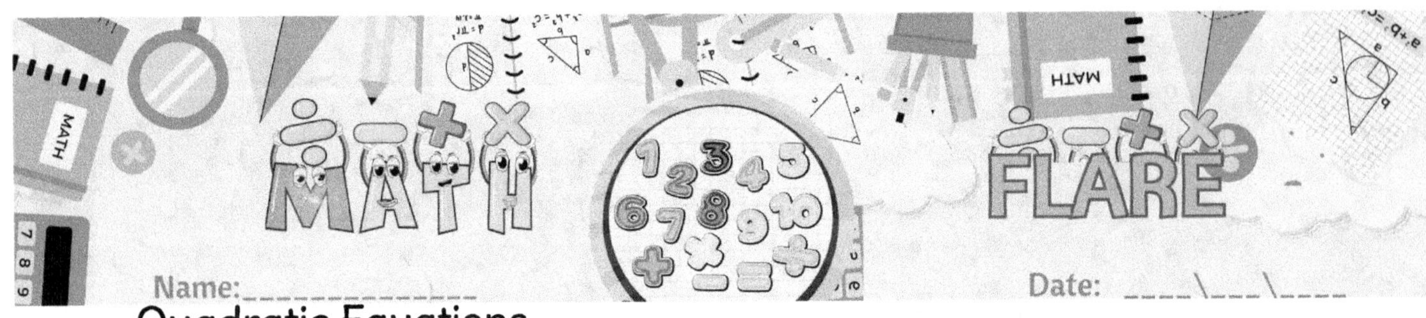

Quadratic Equations

1. $4x^2 - 17 = 0$

2. $-2b^2 + 72 = 0$

3. $-4r^2 - 10r - 4 = 0$

4. $-6r^2 + 7r + 124 = 0$

5. $-2x^2 - 6x + 13 = 0$

6. $-n^2 + 6n + 112 = 0$

7. $9v^2 + 10v - 9 = 0$

8. $7x^2 + 2x - 18 = 0$

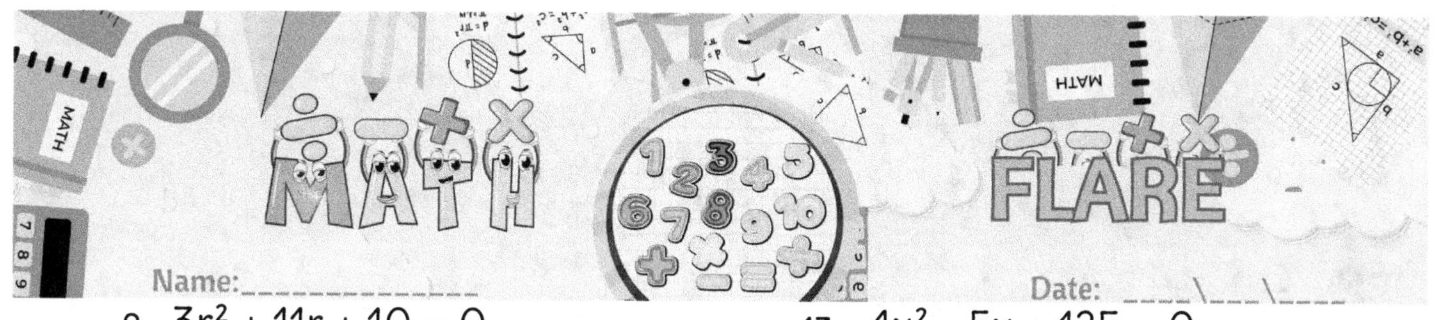

9. $3r^2 + 11r + 10 = 0$

13. $-4x^2 - 5x + 125 = 0$

10. $-12x^2 + 6x - 7 = 0$

14. $-3x^2 + 5x + 138 = 0$

11. $6p^2 + 5p - 144 = 0$

15. $4v^2 - 2v - 17 = 0$

12. $11n^2 - 3n - 13 = 0$

16. $5n^2 + 10n + 3 = 0$

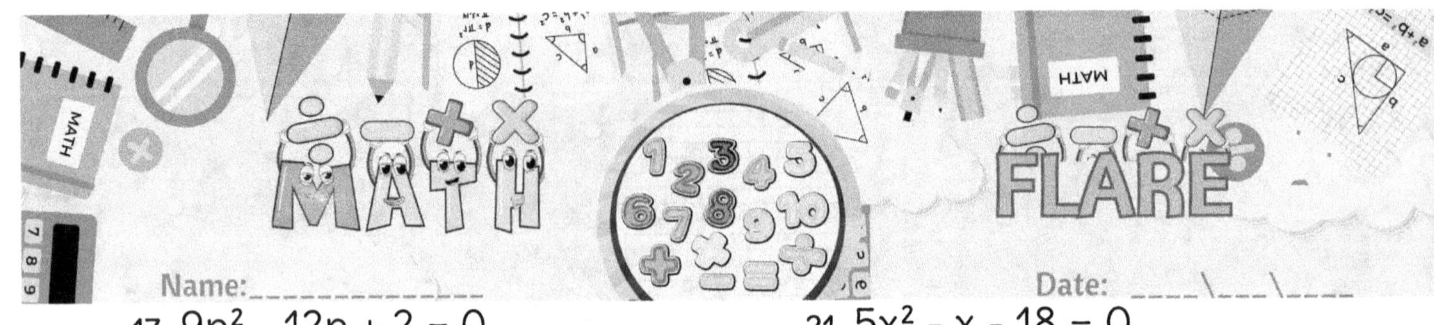

17. $9p^2 - 12p + 2 = 0$

21. $5x^2 - x - 18 = 0$

18. $2m^2 - 32 = 0$

22. $7x^2 + x - 24 = 0$

19. $3b^2 - 8b + 2 = 0$

23. $-11n^2 + 4 = 0$

20. $-7k^2 - 9k + 11 = 0$

24. $-2x^2 - 4x - 2 = 0$

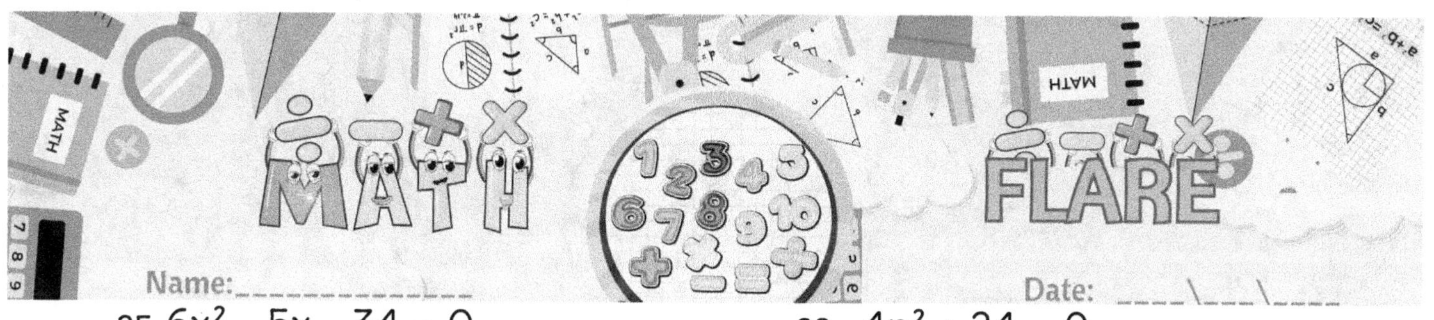

25. $6x^2 - 5x - 34 = 0$

26. $4m^2 + 3 = 0$

27. $m^2 - 144 = 0$

28. $3r^2 - 11r + 10 = 0$

29. $-4p^2 + 24 = 0$

30. $2n^2 - 5n - 63 = 0$

31. $5r^2 + 8r - 29 = -8$

32. $9a^2 - 7a + 18 = 10$

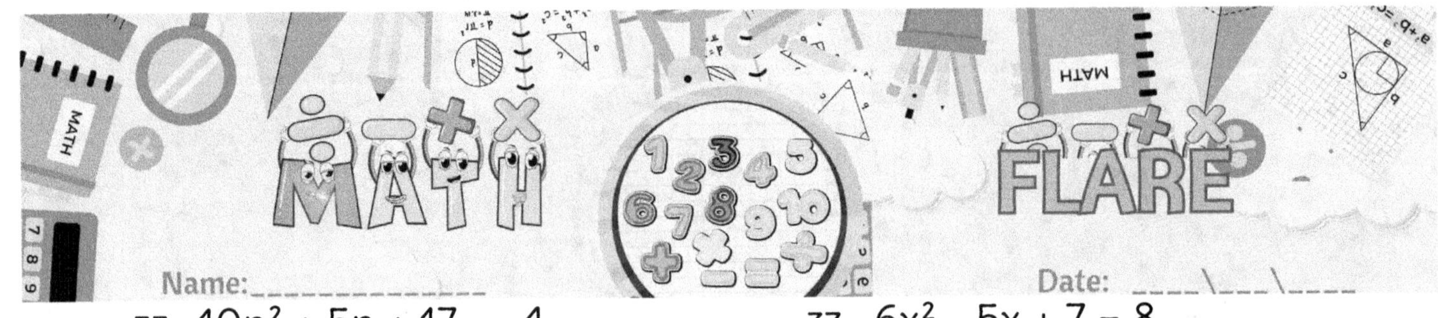

33. $-10n^2 + 5n + 17 = -4$

37. $-6x^2 - 5x + 7 = 8$

34. $6p^2 + 5p - 14 = 11$

38. $-11r^2 - 12r + 15 = -9$

35. $-3x^2 - 9x + 6 = -6$

39. $-3n^2 + 11n + 77 = 7$

36. $-x^2 + 53 = -11$

40. $-10r^2 + 9r + 9 = -8$

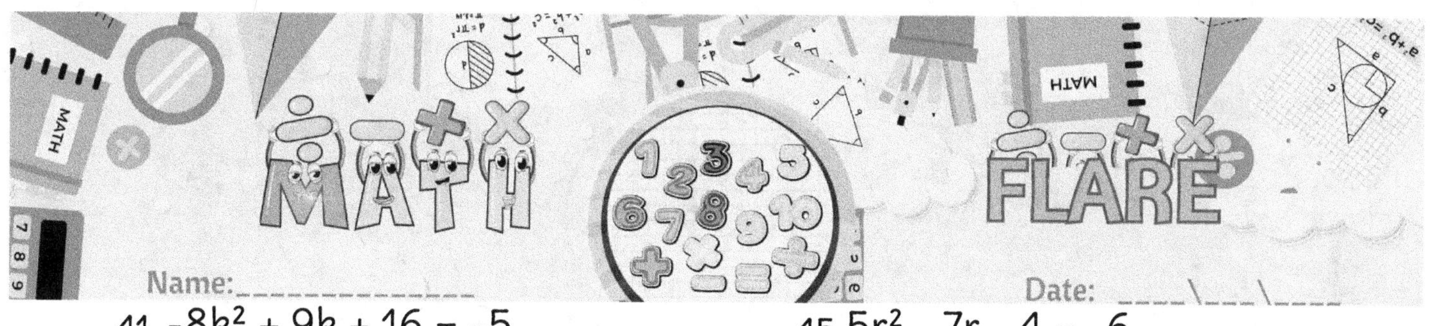

41. $-8k^2 + 9k + 16 = -5$

45. $5r^2 - 7r - 4 = -6$

42. $-9n^2 - 12n + 14 = 7$

46. $2n^2 - 10n - 57 = -9$

43. $b^2 + 11b + 10 = 2$

47. $-8p^2 + 24 = 4$

44. $8x^2 + 3x - 20 = -6$

48. $-n^2 + 5n + 20 = 10$

Name:_____________   Date: _______________

49. $-5x^2 + 3x + 5 = 2$

53. $-4x^2 - 9x + 1 = -8$

50. $-12n^2 - n - 21 = -12$

54. $4n^2 + 4n - 14 = -7$

51. $3x^2 - 9x - 23 = -2$

55. $10x^2 + 3x - 4 = 4$

52. $6m^2 - 11m - 150 = -10$

56. $3k^2 - 11k - 16 = -2$

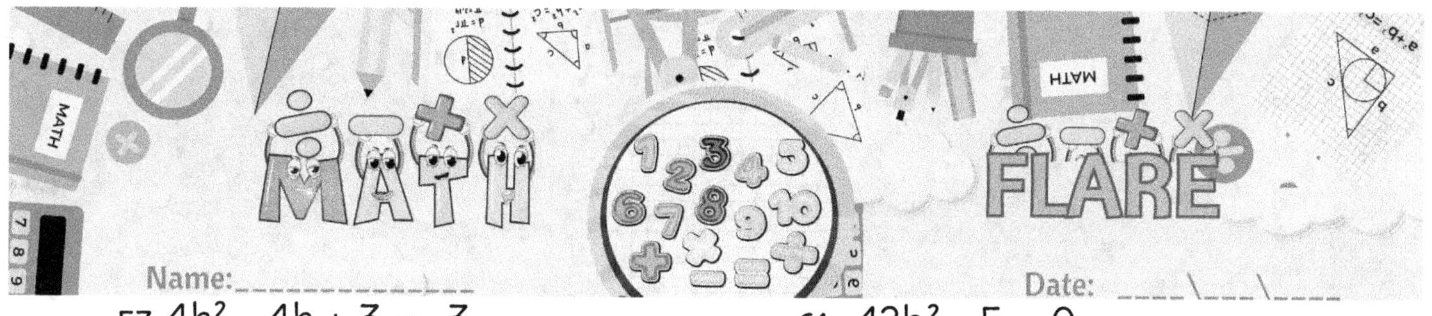

57. $4k^2 - 4k + 3 = -3$

61. $-12b^2 - 5 = 0$

58. $-3v^2 + 12v + 25 = 10$

62. $-4v^2 = -6 + 2v$

59. $3x^2 - 11x - 6 = 10$

63. $9n^2 = -12$

60. $3p^2 + 2 = 12$

64. $8k^2 = 3$

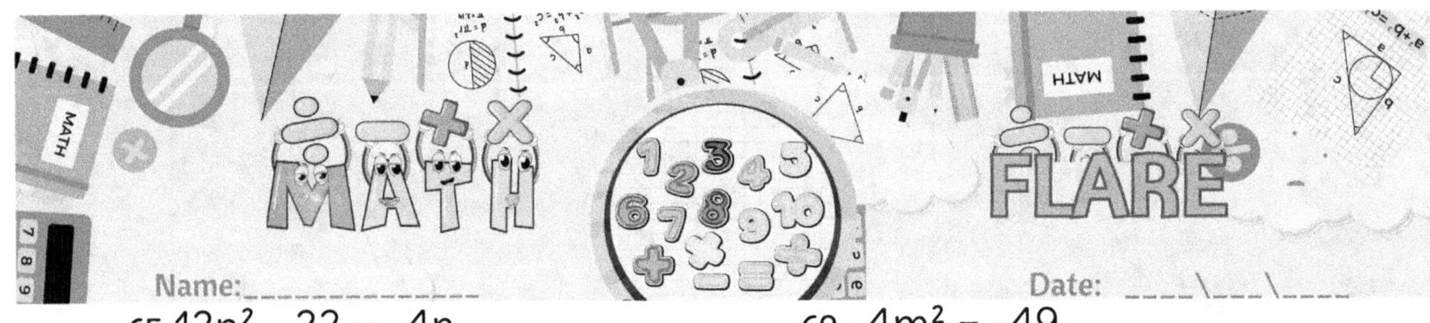

65. $12n^2 - 22 = -4n$

69. $-4m^2 = -49$

66. $x^2 = -6x + 27$

70. $-6v^2 = 12v - 90$

67. $11x^2 + 8x = 21$

71. $-5x^2 = -1 + 2x$

68. $2b^2 - b = 21$

72. $5a^2 = -7a + 6$

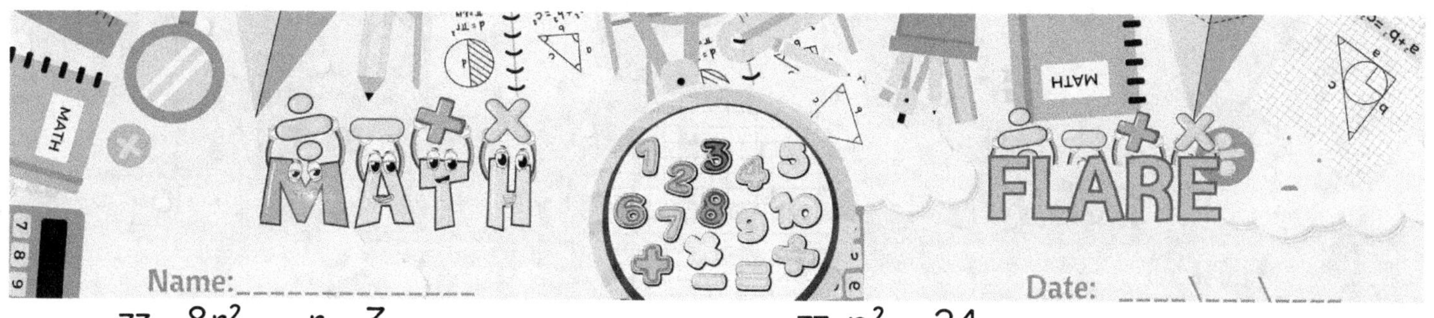

73. $-8r^2 = -r - 3$

77. $p^2 = 24$

74. $v^2 - 5v = 126$

78. $6r^2 - 12r = 17$

75. $7x^2 - 15 = 12x$

79. $-5x^2 = -110 - 3x$

76. $2n^2 - 35 = -9n$

80. $-2n^2 - 7n = 3$

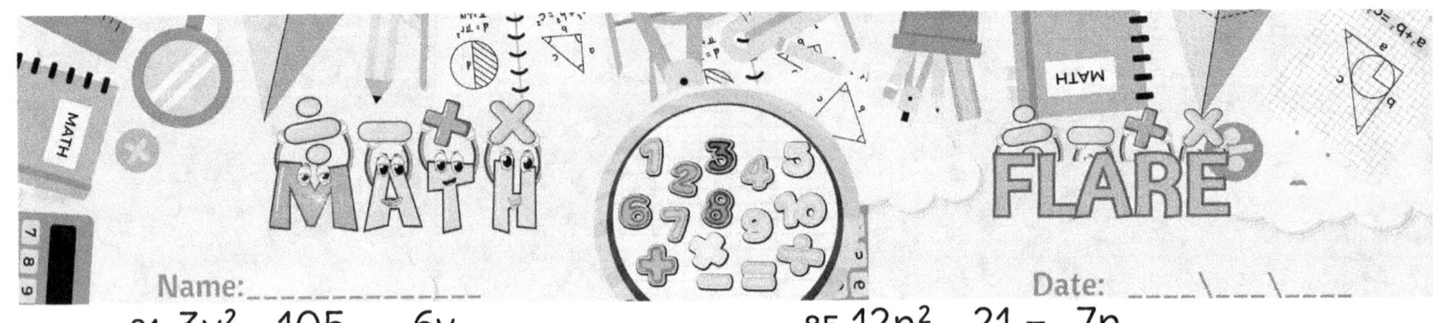

81. $3v^2 - 105 = -6v$

85. $12n^2 - 21 = -7n$

82. $3n^2 = -10n - 5$

86. $-12m^2 + 3 = -4m$

83. $4x^2 = 4x - 7$

87. $2n^2 - 3n = 24$

84. $8x^2 - 13 = 8x$

88. $6n^2 + 8n = 128$

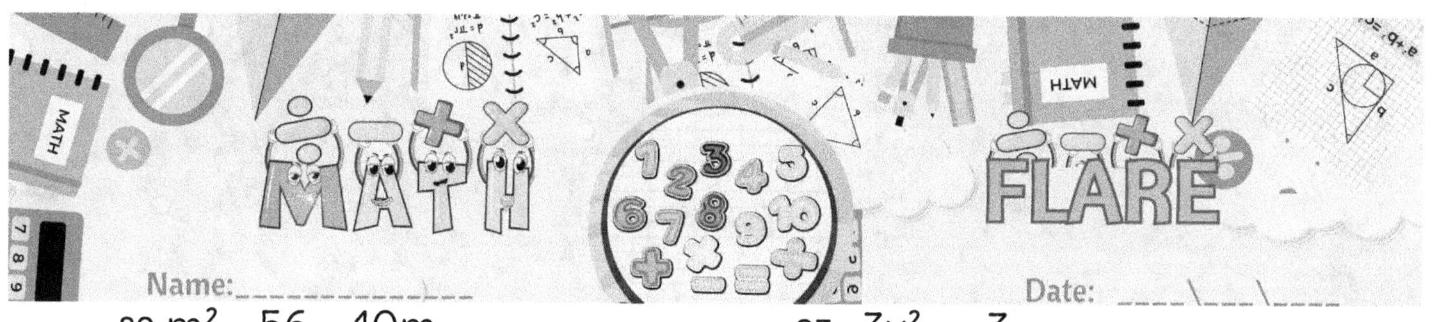

89. $m^2 - 56 = 10m$

93. $-3v^2 = -3$

90. $-10x^2 + 11x = -12$

94. $2a^2 - 3a = 16$

91. $-6x^2 = -24 + 10x$

95. $3n^2 - 4 = 0$

92. $-10x^2 = 10x - 8$

96. $6k^2 + 11k = 112$

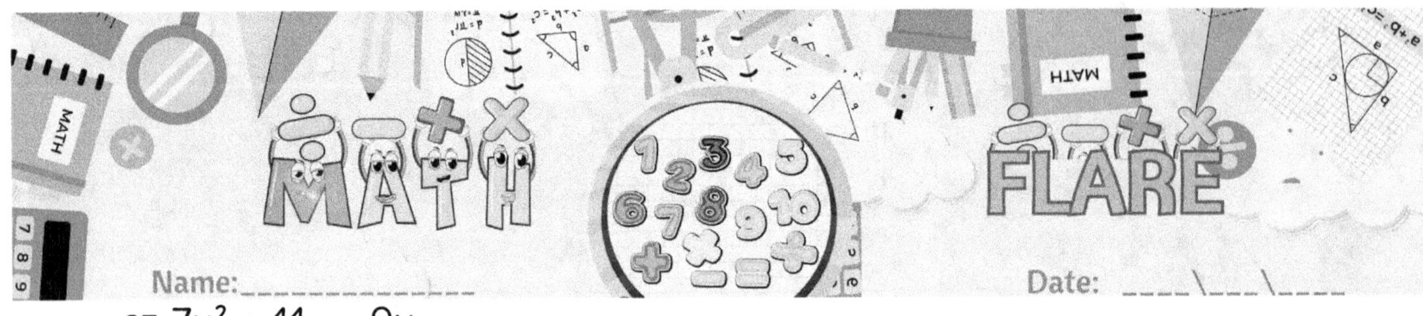

97. $7x^2 + 11 = -9x$

98. $-8n^2 = n + 11$

99. $4a^2 = 144$

100. $-7x^2 = -19$

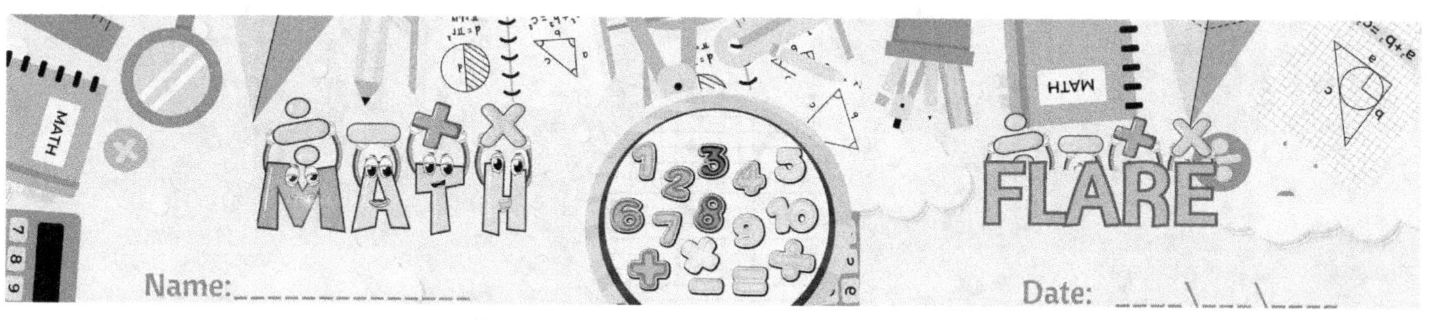

Polynomials: Addition and Subtraction

1. $(3m^2 + 6m^3) + (7m^3 - 6m^2)$

2. $(3k^4 + 5k) + (3k^4 + 8k)$

3. $(v^3 + 2v^2) + (7v^3 + 6v^2)$

4. $(4x + 4) + (8x + 3x^4)$

5. $(4n^3 + 5n^4) + (2n^4 - 5n^3)$

6. $(4p^2 + 4p^3) - (3p^3 - 7p^2)$

7. $(5b^4 + 8) - (2b^4 - 5)$

8. $(2k^3 - k^2) + (7k^3 + 6k^2)$

9. $(4a - 3) + (2a + 2)$

10. $(6 + 7r) + (4 + 4r^3)$

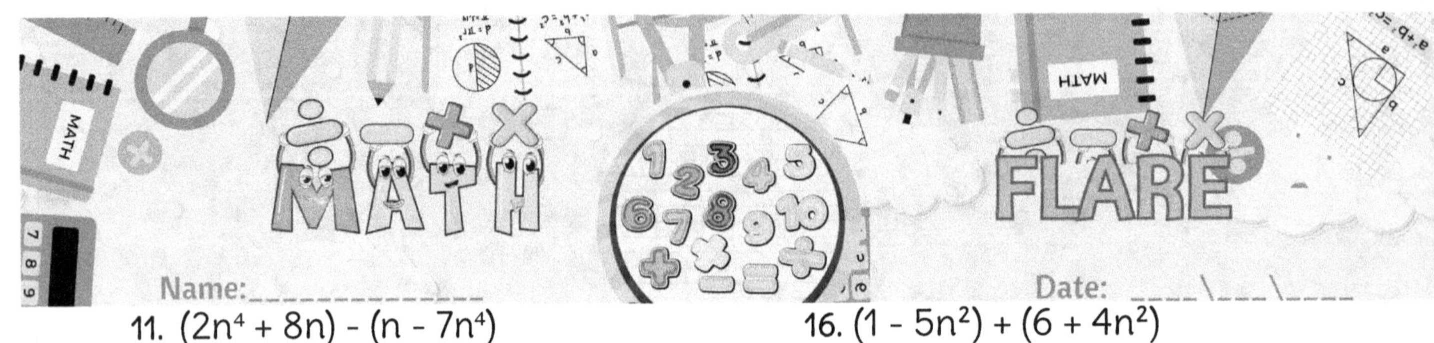

11. $(2n^4 + 8n) - (n - 7n^4)$

16. $(1 - 5n^2) + (6 + 4n^2)$

12. $(5a - 2) + (6a - 2)$

17. $(3 - 4x^4) + (1 - 3x^4)$

13. $(n^2 - 5) - (n^2 - 1)$

18. $(6a^4 + 5a^3) + (2a^4 - 4a^3)$

14. $(5x^2 - 6x^3) + (2x^3 - 3x^2)$

19. $(4p^4 - 4p^3) + (7p^4 - p^3)$

15. $(7 + 5k^2) + (8 - 2k)$

20. $(2n^2 - 6) + (3 + 2n^2)$

21. $(3a^2 - 6a^4) - (8a^4 + a^2)$

26. $(7n - n^2) - (5n + n^2)$

22. $(8n - 3n^3) + (6n^3 - n)$

27. $(p^4 + 6p) - (2p + 4p^4)$

23. $(3v^2 - 7) + (3v^2 - 2)$

28. $(2 - 2x^3) + (6x^3 - 3)$

24. $(4 + x) - (4 + 3x)$

29. $(3r^2 + 8r^3) + (7r^2 + 5r^3)$

25. $(5 - 5x^3) + (8x^3 + 1)$

30. $(4b^4 - 3b^2) - (7b^4 + b^2)$

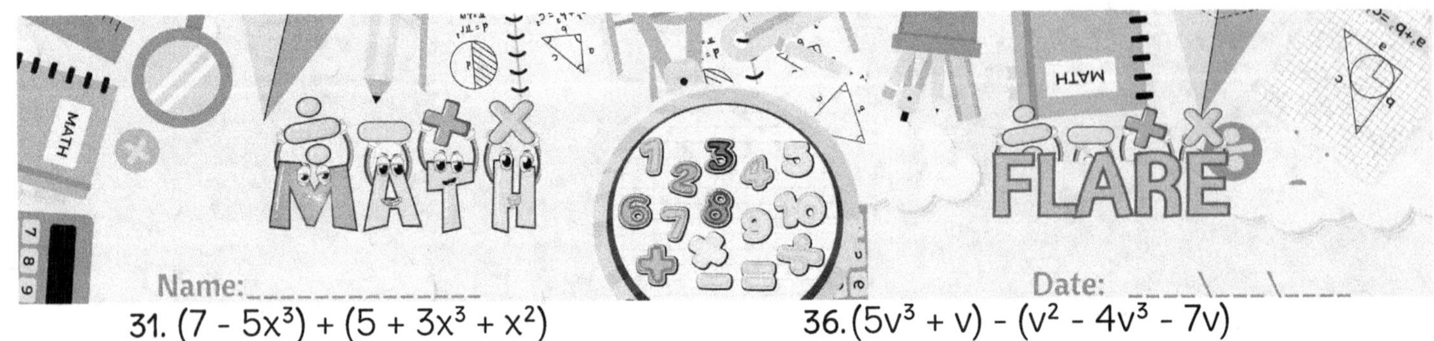

31. $(7 - 5x^3) + (5 + 3x^3 + x^2)$

32. $(1 - n) - (6 - 6n - 6n^4)$

33. $(6 - 6n^4) + (8 - 7n^4 - 3n^2)$

34. $(7x^3 + 6x^4) - (5x^3 + 3x^4 - x^2)$

35. $(2n^3 - 2n^4) + (6n^4 - 2n^2 + 8n^3)$

36. $(5v^3 + v) - (v^2 - 4v^3 - 7v)$

37. $(5 + 2p^2) - (3p^3 + 7p^2 + 1)$

38. $(3k^4 - 3k^2) - (4k^4 + 2k^2 - k)$

39. $(7x^2 - 7x) + (3x^2 - 4 + 4x)$

40. $(6 - k^4) - (k^3 - 3 + 5k^4)$

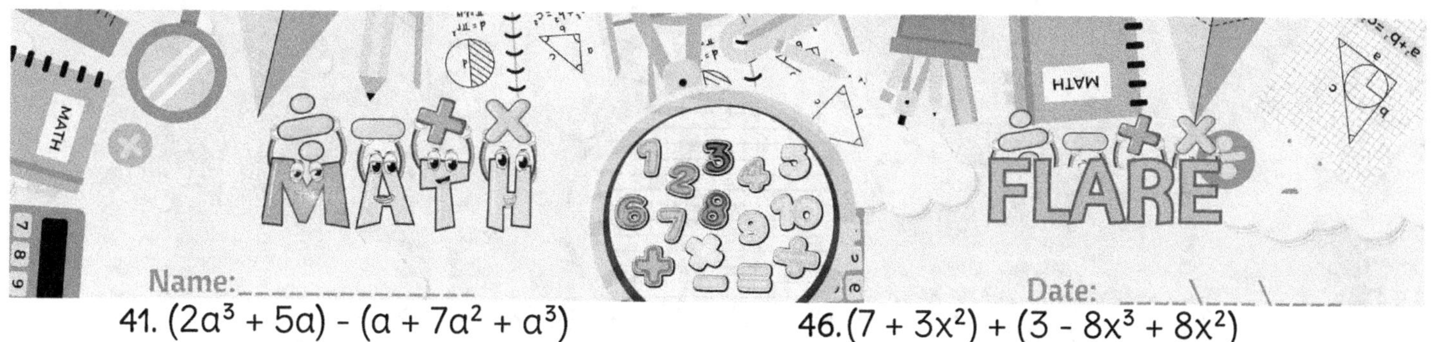

41. $(2a^3 + 5a) - (a + 7a^2 + a^3)$

42. $(2x^2 + 3x) - (8x - 7x^2 + 4x^3)$

43. $(4x^4 + 2) + (5x + 8 + 4x^4)$

44. $(3x - 7x^2) + (8x - 2x^3 - x^2)$

45. $(3x^2 - 8x) + (3x - 8x^2 + 7x^3)$

46. $(7 + 3x^2) + (3 - 8x^3 + 8x^2)$

47. $(x^3 + 8) + (6 - 6x^3 + 8x^2)$

48. $(5x^3 + x^4) - (8x + 7x^3 + 5x^4)$

49. $(6n^3 - 5n) + (7n + 3n^3 - 2)$

50. $(8a^2 - 4a^4) - (3a^2 - 3a^4 - 4a^3)$

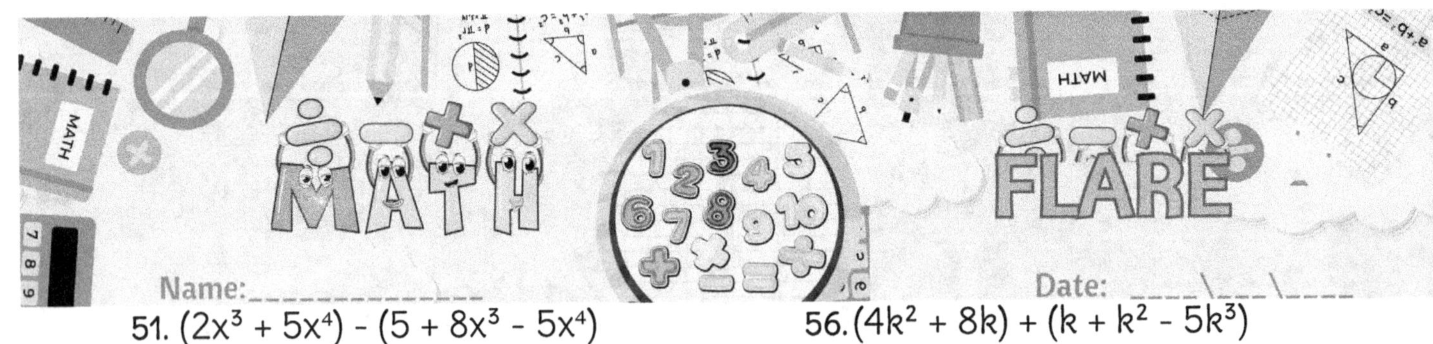

51. $(2x^3 + 5x^4) - (5 + 8x^3 - 5x^4)$

52. $(7a^2 - 1) - (8a^4 - 5 - 4a^2)$

53. $(5 - 6x^2) - (6x^2 - 7x + 7)$

54. $(4x^2 - 4x^3) + (4x^3 + 7x^2 - 8x)$

55. $(5 + 2n^2) + (1 + 5n^4 - 8n^2)$

56. $(4k^2 + 8k) + (k + k^2 - 5k^3)$

57. $(x^2 + x^3) - (7x - 6x^2 + 3x^3)$

58. $(6n^2 - 8n^3) + (4n^3 + 7n^2 + 5n^4)$

59. $(6v^2 + 8) + (2v^2 + 7 - 5v^3)$

60. $(6b^3 - b) + (4b^3 + 2b - 4b^4)$

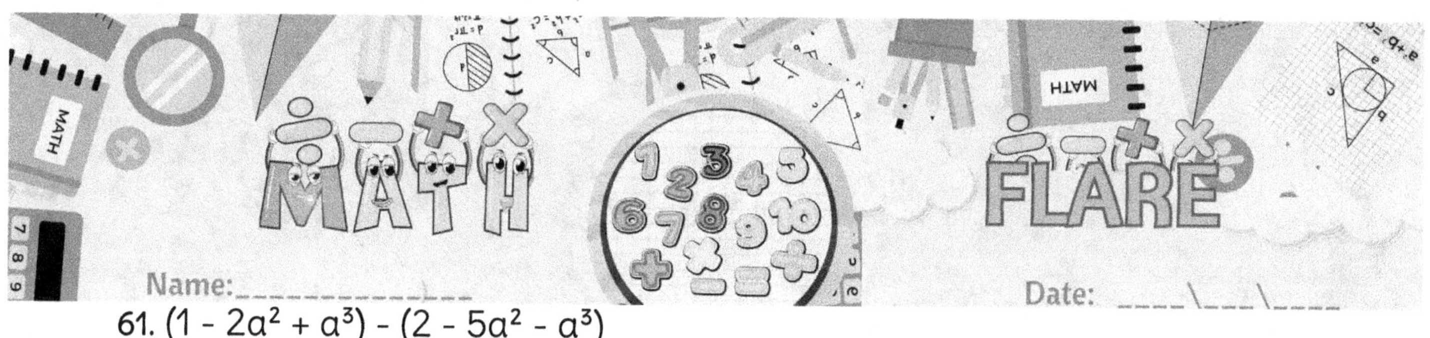

Name:________________________   Date: _______________

61. $(1 - 2a^2 + a^3) - (2 - 5a^2 - a^3)$

62. $(4 - 2a^4 + 2a^3) + (6a^3 + 5a^2 - 4)$

63. $(3 + 4a^2 - 2a^3) - (7 - a^2 - 7a^3)$

64. $(5x + 6 + 6x^4) - (2x^3 - 8x^4 - 5x)$

65. $(3p^2 + 4p^4 + 3p) - (7p - 4p^2 + 2p^4)$

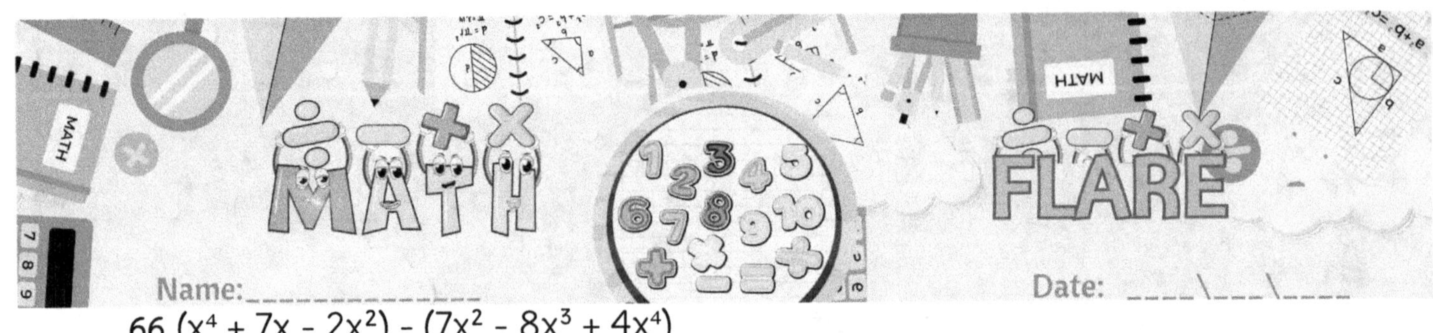

66. $(x^4 + 7x - 2x^2) - (7x^2 - 8x^3 + 4x^4)$

67. $(8v^3 - 3v^4 + 3) + (v - 7v^3 + 8v^4)$

68. $(5 + 7p - p^3) + (2p + 5p^3 + 7)$

69. $(5x - 2x^4 + 2x^2) + (4x - 2x^2 + 5x^4)$

70. $(2x^3 - x - 6x^2) - (7x^2 - 7 + 4x)$

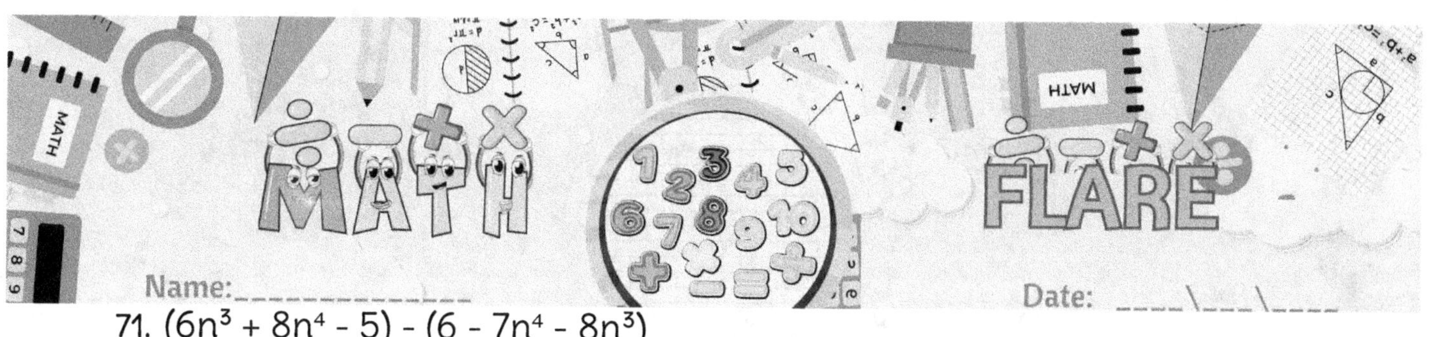

71. $(6n^3 + 8n^4 - 5) - (6 - 7n^4 - 8n^3)$

72. $(3v^3 + 8v - 4v^2) + (5v + 8v^2 - 7v^3)$

73. $(2v^3 + 5v^2 - 6v) + (v^3 - v^2 - v)$

74. $(6n^3 + 6 - 3n) - (2 + 8n + 2n^3)$

75. $(7v + 3v^3 - 3) + (8v^3 - 2v^2 - 6v)$

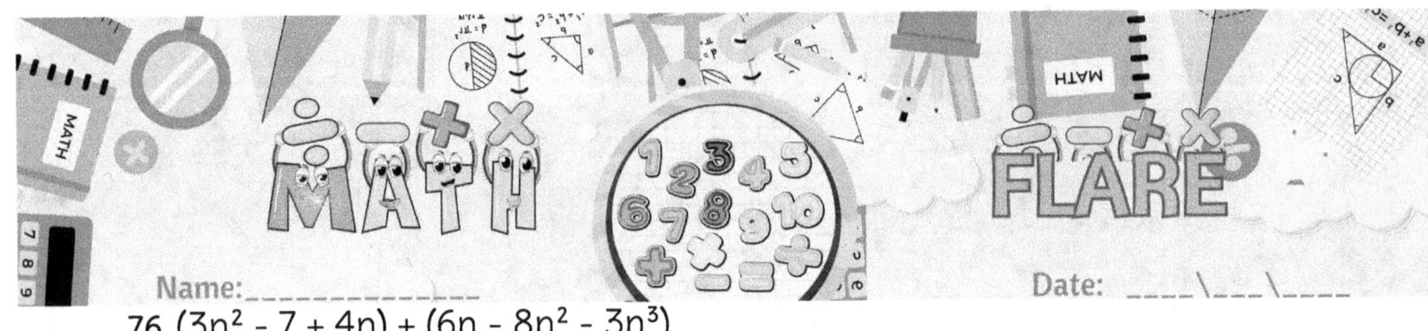

76. $(3n^2 - 7 + 4n) + (6n - 8n^2 - 3n^3)$

77. $(5x + 2x^3 - 5) - (6x - 4x^4 - 8x^3)$

78. $(8x^2 + 8x^4 - x) - (7x^2 - 7x^4 + 6x)$

79. $(6x - 8x^2 - 3x^4) + (x^2 - 7x + 6x^4)$

80. $(5n^4 + 4n^3 - 5n^2) - (3n - 5n^2 + n^3)$

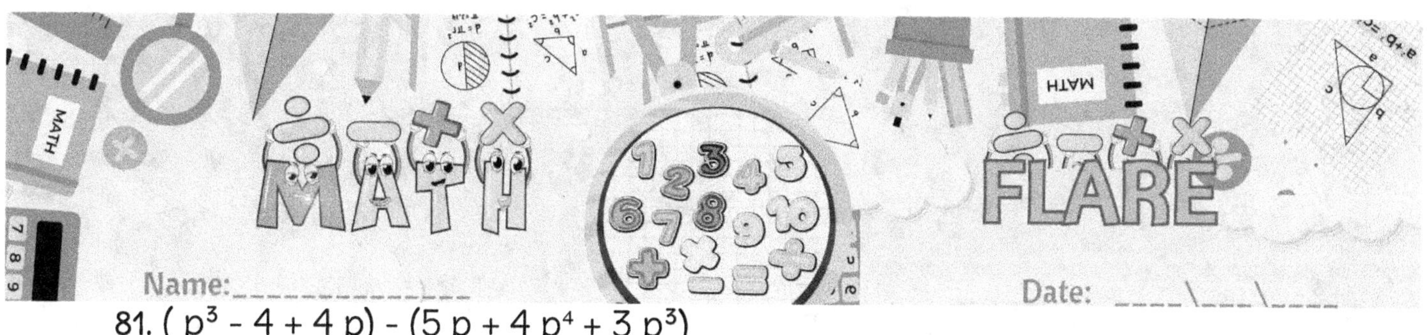

81. $(p^3 - 4 + 4p) - (5p + 4p^4 + 3p^3)$

82. $(6v^4 - 4v - 5) + (v^4 - 4 - v)$

83. $(8p^2 - 6p^4 + 4p^3) - (8p^4 + 7 - 3p^2)$

84. $(1 - n^3 + 3n^4) + (n + 4n^4 - 4n^3)$

85. $(4 - 8v^2 - v^3) + (7v^2 + 2 + 4v^3)$

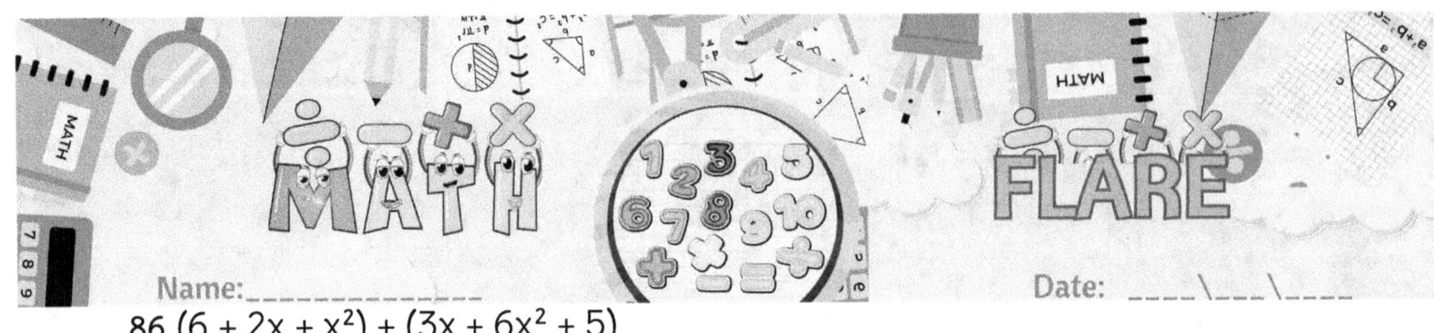

86. $(6 + 2x + x^2) + (3x + 6x^2 + 5)$

87. $(5n + 3n^2 + 2) - (2 + 2n^2 - n)$

88. $(3a + 2a^3 - 7a^4) + (3a + 2 + 8a^3)$

89. $(4b + 5 + 5b^4) - (4 + 8b^4 + 7b)$

90. $(6 - 2x^3 - x) + (3x + 1 + 8x^2)$

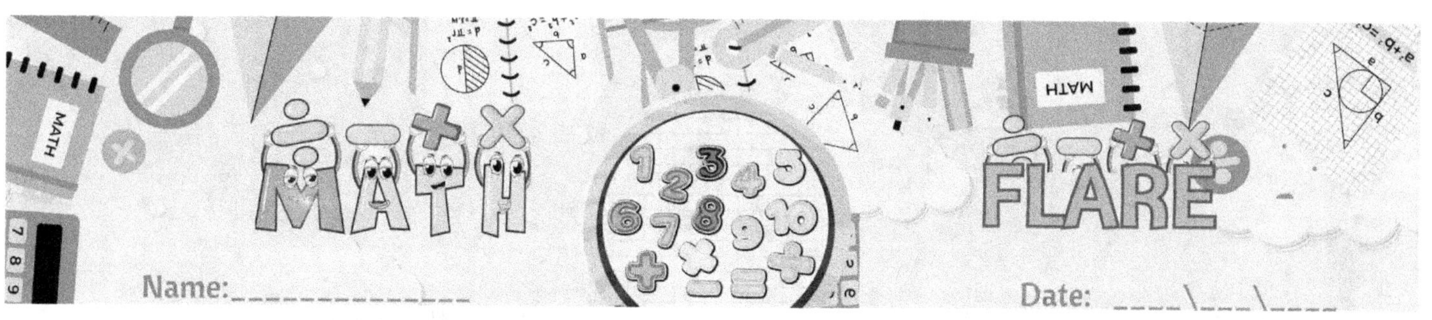

Polynomials: Multiplication

1. (2x + 4 y)(5x - 7 y)

2. (a - 2b)(5a - 5b)

3. (7x + 2 y)(x - 6 y)

4. (8a - 4b)(4a - 2b)

5. (x - 5 y)(8x - 7 y)

6. (4u + 4v)(u + 3v)

7. (5x - y)(5x + 4 y)

8. (3a - 6b)(a - 7b)

9. (7a - 7b)(5a - 6b)

10. (6x - 3 y)(7x - 7 y)

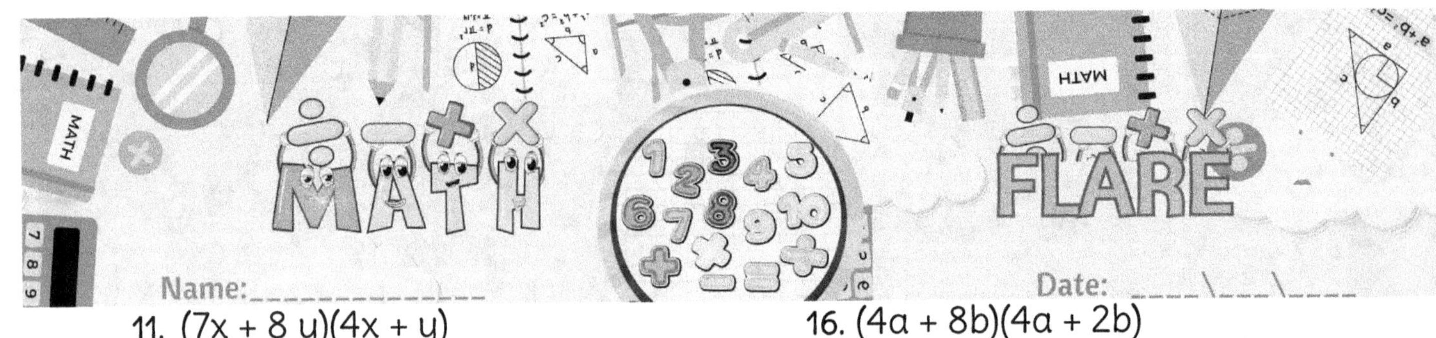

11. $(7x + 8y)(4x + y)$

16. $(4a + 8b)(4a + 2b)$

12. $(6m + 5n)(m + 8n)$

17. $(x - 6y)(4x + 5y)$

13. $(2a + 6b)(7a + 3b)$

18. $(5a + 7b)(2a - 5b)$

14. $(6x - y)(8x + 3y)$

19. $(3a + b)(2a + 3b)$

15. $(2x + 3y)(6x - 3y)$

20. $(7x - 6y)(5x - 3y)$

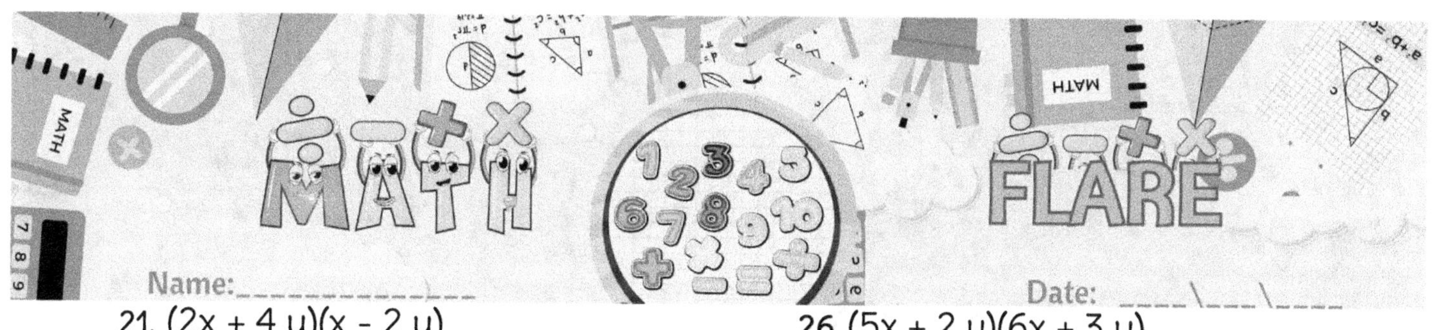

21. $(2x + 4y)(x - 2y)$

22. $(5a - 4b)(6a + 3b)$

23. $(5x - 5y)(8x - 6y)$

24. $(8m + 7n)(5m - 5n)$

25. $(u + 2v)(2u - 2v)$

26. $(5x + 2y)(6x + 3y)$

27. $(3x + 7y)(5x + 7y)$

28. $(2x - 8y)(8x - 3y)$

29. $(8x + 4y)(3x - 4y)$

30. $(3x - 2y)(5x + 6y)$

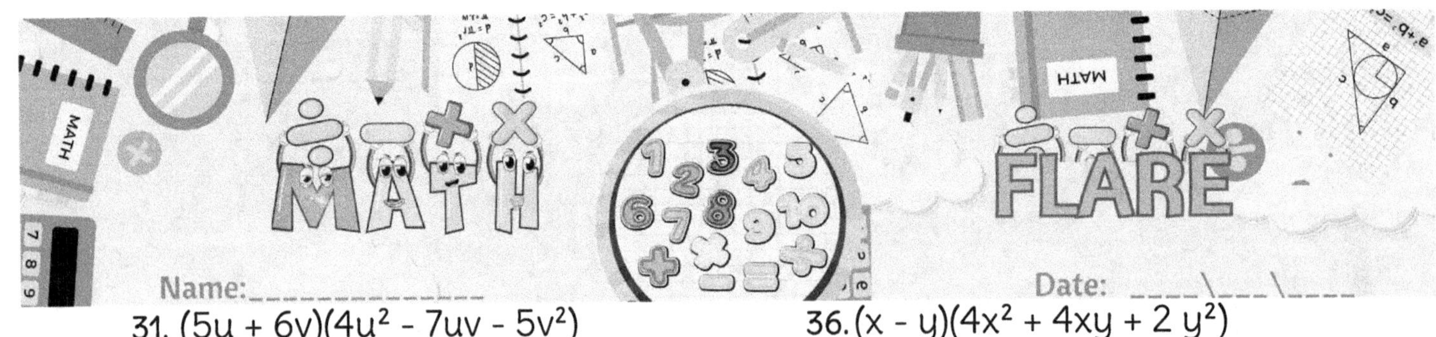

31. $(5u + 6v)(4u^2 - 7uv - 5v^2)$

36. $(x - y)(4x^2 + 4xy + 2y^2)$

32. $(3x - 2y)(x^2 + 7xy + 6y^2)$

37. $(5u + v)(7u^2 - uv + 2v^2)$

33. $(7a - 8b)(7a^2 - ab + b^2)$

38. $(8x - 7y)(3x^2 + 8xy + 6y^2)$

34. $(6a - 4b)(6a^2 - 8ab + 7b^2)$

39. $(m - 4n)(m^2 + 3mn + 8n^2)$

35. $(6u - 2v)(7u^2 - 3uv - 7v^2)$

40. $(4a + 6b)(a^2 + 8ab - 3b^2)$

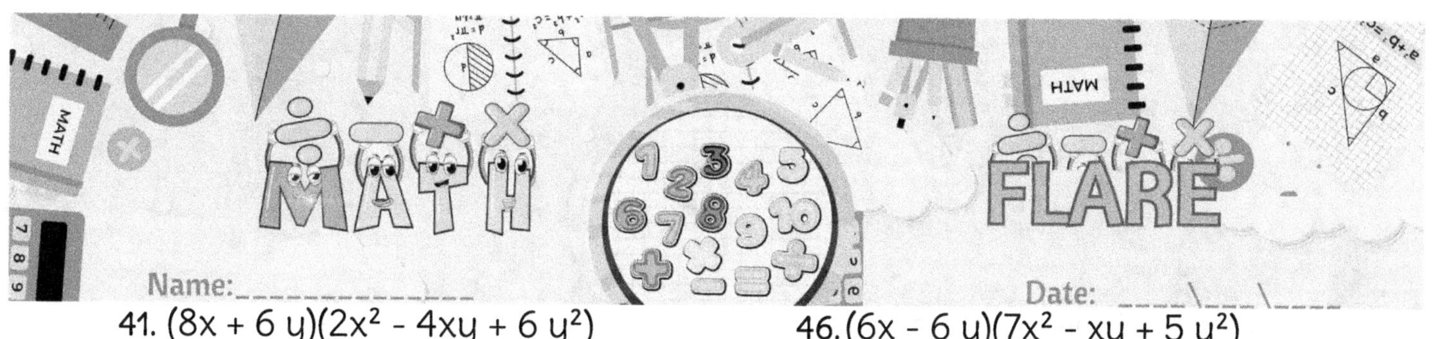

41. $(8x + 6y)(2x^2 - 4xy + 6y^2)$

46. $(6x - 6y)(7x^2 - xy + 5y^2)$

42. $(5x + 8y)(6x^2 - 6xy + 7y^2)$

47. $(3u - 5v)(2u^2 - 7uv + 5v^2)$

43. $(5m - n)(8m^2 + 5mn - n^2)$

48. $(3a + b)(7a^2 - 7ab + 4b^2)$

44. $(5x - 6y)(x^2 - 7xy - 5y^2)$

49. $(7x - 3y)(7x^2 - 4xy + 7y^2)$

45. $(4x - 5y)(8x^2 + 4xy + 8y^2)$

50. $(4x + 3y)(3x^2 + 4xy + y^2)$

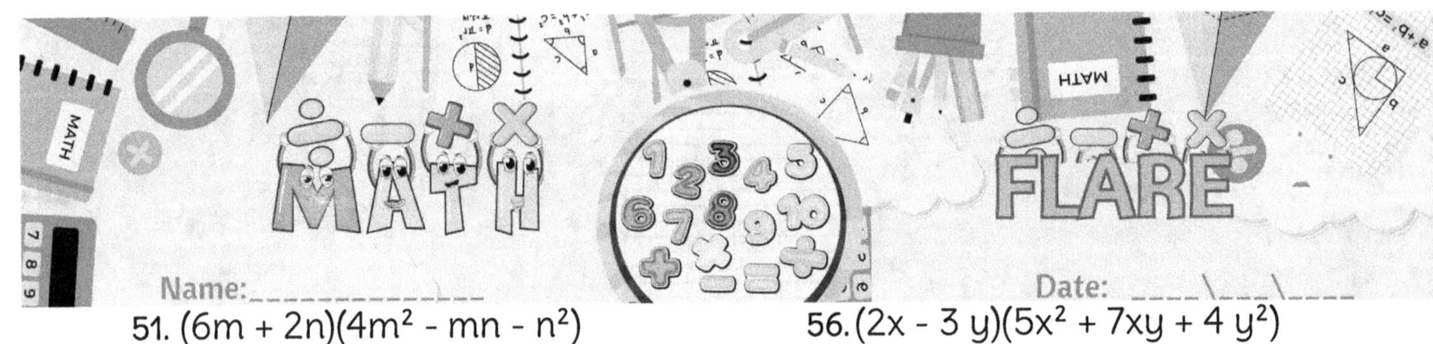

51. $(6m + 2n)(4m^2 - mn - n^2)$

56. $(2x - 3y)(5x^2 + 7xy + 4y^2)$

52. $(2x - 6y)(4x^2 - xy + y^2)$

57. $(2x + y)(x^2 - 4xy - 8y^2)$

53. $(x + 2y)(7x^2 + 8xy + 2y^2)$

58. $(4a - 6b)(5a^2 - 3ab + b^2)$

54. $(5m - 2n)(7m^2 - 6mn - 7n^2)$

59. $(7a + 6b)(6a^2 + 6ab - 7b^2)$

55. $(5x - 5y)(4x^2 + 3xy - 2y^2)$

60. $(4x + 6y)(4x^2 - 2xy - y^2)$

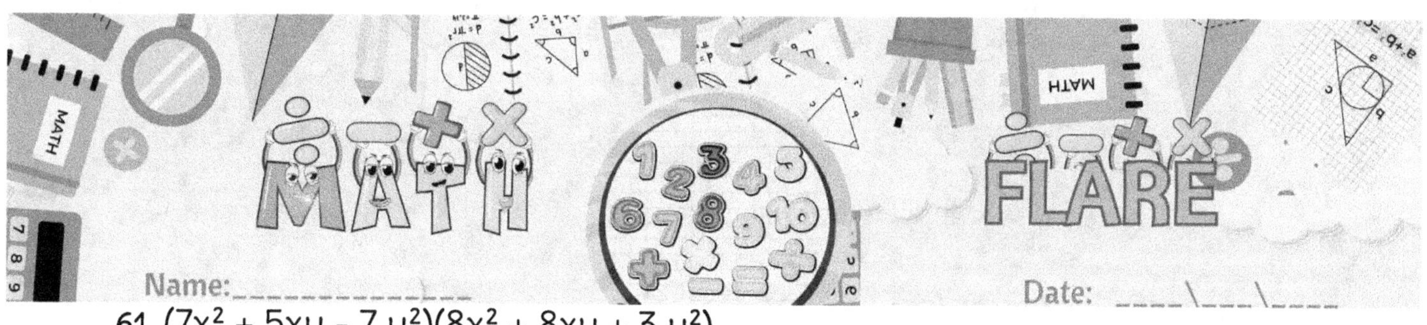

61. $(7x^2 + 5xy - 7y^2)(8x^2 + 8xy + 3y^2)$

62. $(3x^2 - 3xy - 8y^2)(8x^2 + 6xy - 2y^2)$

63. $(3a^2 + 5ab + 2b^2)(8a^2 + 6ab + 7b^2)$

64. $(3x^2 - 7xy - 8y^2)(2x^2 - 7xy + 6y^2)$

65. $(6u^2 + 5uv + v^2)(7u^2 - 8uv - 4v^2)$

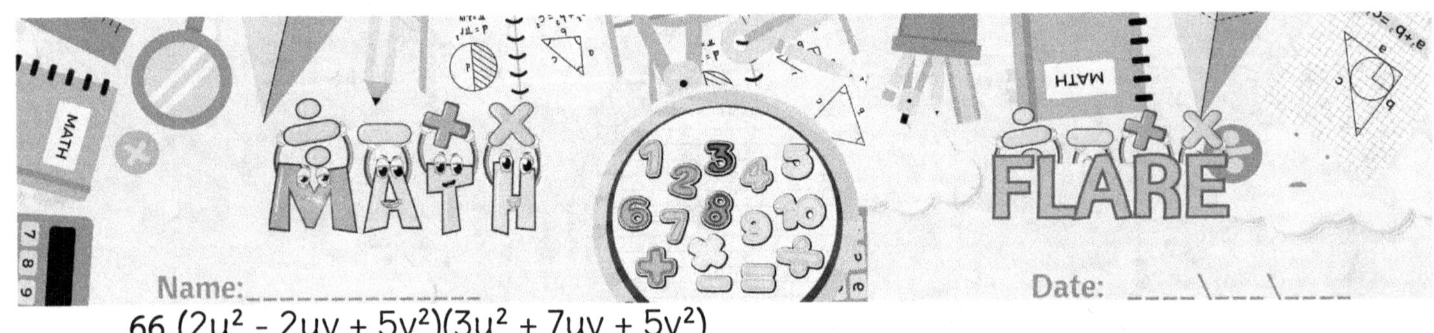

66. $(2u^2 - 2uv + 5v^2)(3u^2 + 7uv + 5v^2)$

67. $(3a^2 - 8ab - 8b^2)(7a^2 + 7ab + 4b^2)$

68. $(2m^2 - mn - n^2)(7m^2 + 8mn - n^2)$

69. $(7m^2 - 4mn - 3n^2)(5m^2 + 4mn - 6n^2)$

70. $(8x^2 - 8xy - 5y^2)(3x^2 + xy - 5y^2)$

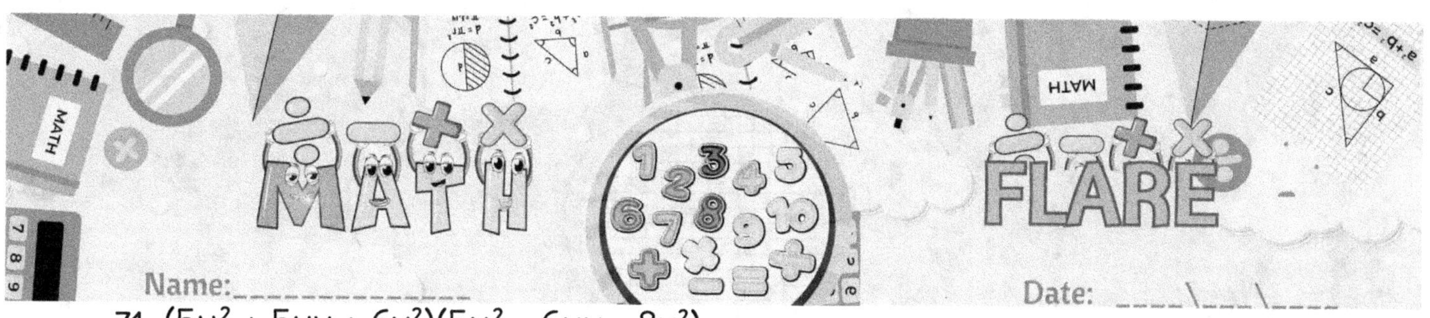

71. $(5u^2 + 5uv + 6v^2)(5u^2 - 6uv - 8v^2)$

72. $(2u^2 - 8uv - 6v^2)(2u^2 - uv + v^2)$

73. $(2x^2 + xy + 5 y^2)(6x^2 - 3xy - 8 y^2)$

74. $(6x^2 - xy - 4 y^2)(2x^2 + 8xy - 2 y^2)$

75. $(6x^2 + 4xy - 2 y^2)(x^2 - 7xy - 3 y^2)$

76. $(6x^2 - 5xy - y^2)(6x^2 + xy + 3y^2)$

77. $(x^2 - 6xy - 2y^2)(3x^2 - xy + 3y^2)$

78. $(3x^2 + 3xy + 8y^2)(5x^2 - 5xy + 7y^2)$

79. $(3u^2 - 4uv + 7v^2)(4u^2 - 7uv - 7v^2)$

80. $(3x^2 + 5xy + 6y^2)(7x^2 - 2xy - 3y^2)$

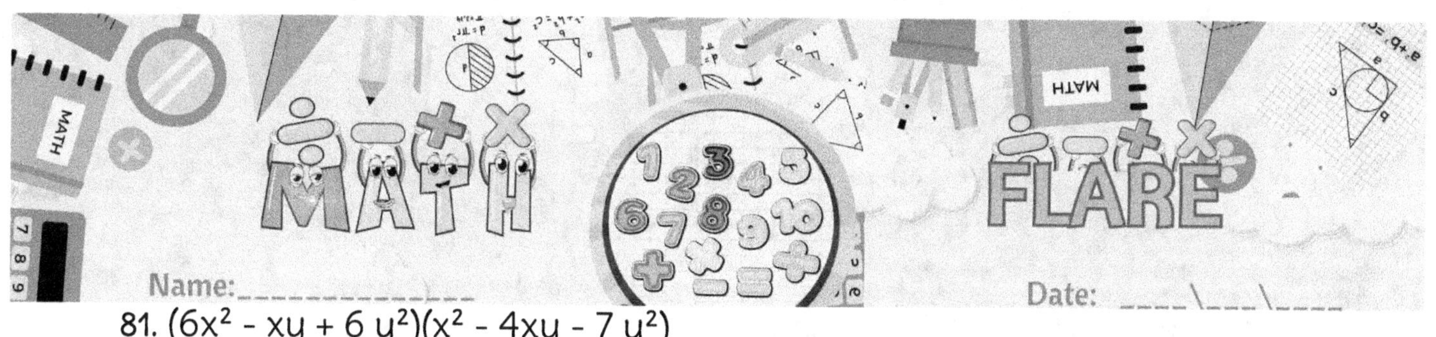

81. $(6x^2 - xy + 6y^2)(x^2 - 4xy - 7y^2)$

82. $(2a^2 - 2ab - 2b^2)(4a^2 + 4ab + 5b^2)$

83. $(a^2 - 5ab - 3b^2)(5a^2 - 2ab + 5b^2)$

84. $(2m^2 + mn + n^2)(4m^2 - 7mn + 2n^2)$

85. $(6x^2 - 2xy + 7y^2)(5x^2 + 6xy - y^2)$

86. $(7m^2 - 7mn - 7n^2)(8m^2 + 6mn - 8n^2)$

87. $(2x^2 - 6xy - 5y^2)(x^2 - 2xy + y^2)$

88. $(8x^2 - xy + 7y^2)(8x^2 - 8xy + 2y^2)$

89. $(2x^2 - 7xy - 4y^2)(6x^2 + 7xy - 8y^2)$

90. $(3a^2 + ab - 6b^2)(8a^2 - 4ab + 3b^2)$

ANSWERS

Page 1: Equations: (One Side)

1. x = 1	2. z = 16	3. z = 12	4. x = 13	5. x = 0
6. k = -6	7. m = -3	8. z = 13	9. m = 20	10. z = 3
11. x = 14	12. z = 15	13. x = -10	14. y = -2	15. x = 6
16. k = 27	17. y = -48	18. m = -6	19. z = 1	20. k = 2
21. m = -10	22. z = -1	23. y = -5	24. m = -8	25. x = 4
26. y = 0	27. y = -8	28. m = -6	29. z = 19	30. k = -7
31. m = 60	32. y = -7	33. k = 5	34. x = 11	35. z = -8
36. z = 18	37. z = 19	38. k = 10	39. y = 14	40. z = -45
41. k = 14	42. x = -5	43. k = 16	44. k = 0	45. k = 3
46. m = 7	47. y = -4	48. k = -10	49. z = 1	50. z = 4
51. z = 10	52. z = 17	53. m = 7	54. y = 2	55. x = 8
56. x = 20				

Page 8: Equations: (Two Sides)

1. m = 5	2. a = 6	3. s = 4	4. x = 2	5. m = -9
6. b = -2	7. y = -8	8. m = 6	9. y = -6	10. a = 8
11. k = -7	12. k = 4	13. x = -10	14. y = -10	15. b = -5
16. z = 1	17. k = 7	18. x = -6	19. b = -2	20. s = 5
21. a = 8	22. x = -1	23. m = 5	24. x = -8	25. y = -8
26. m = 1	27. s = -2	28. m = 6	29. k = 7	30. k = -8

31. x = -10   32. k = -9   33. s = -5   34. a = 9   35. z = 5

36. a = -7   37. a = -9   38. x = -10   39. k = 4   40. m = 6

41. m = 1   42. a = -10   43. a = 9   44. a = 10   45. s = 6

46. x = -1   47. k = -4   48. k = -4   49. b = 8   50. k = -5

51. x = 1   52. k = 1   53. k = -2   54. z = -6   55. k = 10

56. x = 2

Page 15: Solving One-Step Equations

1. 8   2. 5   3. 2   4. 1   5. 6   6. 8   7. 8   8. 3   9. 6

10. 6   11. 6   12. 3   13. 6   14. 6   15. 5   16. 6   17. 3   18. 1

19. 4   20. 4   21. 10   22. 9   23. 10   24. 3   25. 8   26. 8   27. 10

28. 9   29. 8   30. 6   31. 7   32. 3   33. 8   34. 7   35. 9   36. 10

37. 7   38. 1   39. 9   40. 8   41. 5   42. 1   43. 4   44. 7   45. 10

46. 6   47. 5   48. 4   49. 10   50. 8   51. 7   52. 3   53. 4   54. 8

55. 7   56. 8

Page 22: Solving Two-Step Equations

1. 10   2. 9   3. 9   4. 10   5. 10   6. 5   7. 10   8. 9   9. 8

10. 7   11. 8   12. 10   13. 1   14. 2   15. 10   16. 1   17. 1   18. 1

19. 7   20. 2   21. 4   22. 5   23. 1   24. 5   25. 8   26. 8   27. 4

28. 4   29. 7   30. 5   31. 1   32. 2   33. 4   34. 6   35. 8   36. 10

37. 10   38. 8   39. 3   40. 1   41. 8   42. 10   43. 4   44. 3   45. 2

46. 7   47. 6   48. 6   49. 2   50. 2   51. 9   52. 8   53. 10   54. 5

55. 6   56. 7

Page 29: Solving Multi-Step Equations

1. 7	2. 5	39. 1	40. 6
3. 10	4. 10	41. 4	42. 7
5. 9	6. 3	43. 4	44. 1 or -199 or ...
7. 4	8. 1	45. 5 or -199 or ...	46. 6
9. 6	10. 1	47. 8	48. 9
11. 7	12. 5	49. 6	50. 1
13. 6	14. 5	51. 7	52. 2
15. 8	16. 4	53. 7	54. 8
17. 10	18. 3	55. 1	56. 1
19. 9	20. 10		
21. 4	22. 1		
23. 5	24. 5		
25. 5	26. 8		
27. 7	28. 4		
29. 9	30. 5		
31. 9	32. 1		
33. 1	34. 10		
35. 10	36. 7		
37. 9	38. 1		

Page 36: Distributing and Combining Terms

1. -2x - 2
2. 18b
3. x - 2
4. n
5. -3x
6. 8r
7. -8a
8. 7r
9. -2x
10. 7n - 2
11. -10 p + 4
12. 40 + 90m
13. -10a - 35
14. -81b - 36
15. 14n + 49
16. -16 p - 16
17. 20x + 8
18. 7 - 56x
19. -5 - 30x
20. -45b - 35
21. -1 + 28a
22. -27x + 4
23. 19 - 40a
24. 2k
25. 35 - 24m
26. -6m + 3
27. 57 - 30m
28. 60x + 21
29. 9 - 40x
30. 40k - 54
31. 74x
32. 18x - 20
33. -58 + 2 p
34. 41 - 34v
35. 78 - 15r
36. -37 - 44m
37. -110 - 66m
38. 26 - 82x
39. 21x + 60
40. 57r + 18
41. $64n - 42n^2 - 8$
42. $33k^2 - 13k$
43. $-17n + 2n^2 - 20$
44. $8r + 15r^2 + 6$
45. 20x + 40
46. 47x + 36
47. $20v + 30 + 7v^2$
48. $4m^2 - 34m - 14$
49. $-49 p^2 + 38 p - 12$
50. -12
51. -39 + 16x
52. -1 + 27m
53. -6k - 27
54. 36n - 5
55. -22 p + 12
56. -30k + 13
57. 43 p - 16
58. -22 - 99x
59. 20x - 8
60. 4 - 18x
61. 2k - 20
62. -2 - 41 p
63. -15x - 5
64. 20n - 21
65. -16n + 22
66. -14 - 20b
67. -20x - 2
68. -4 - 4x
69. 12a + 16
70. -15n - 39

Page 43: Factoring with Special Cases

1. $8(5n^3 - 1)$
2. $8(3b^2 + 1)$
3. $10r^3(4r^2 - 7)$
4. $-6x(3x^5 + 2)$
5. $-5(1 + 9p)$
6. $7(5m^3 - 2)$
7. $-5(8 + 7b^3)$
8. $5(5n + 2)$
9. $9n(-6n + 1)$
10. $8x(8 - 9x)$
11. $x^2y^5(4xy^2 - 3)$
12. $a^5b^6(2 - 3a^2b)$
13. $3x(1 + xy)$
14. $6ab^9(3b^5 + 2a^2)$
15. $7x^2(-8y^2 + 7)$
16. $-7x^3y(2y^4 + 9)$
17. $x^2y(6x^2y - 1)$
18. $-8n(6m^2 + 7)$
19. $7x(-4y^5 + 3x)$
20. $4x(5y - 9x)$
21. $6b(2 - 2b^2 + 3b^3)$
22. $8b(2b^3 + 3b + 8)$
23. $10k^2(4k^2 - 5k + 9)$
24. $6x(-9x^3 - 8 + 9x^2)$
25. $-6x(3x^2 + x + 5)$
26. $10n^2(-4n^3 + 3n + 4)$
27. $5(-4 + 6x + 5x^2)$
28. $n(7n^3 + 9n^2 + 2)$
29. $6n^4(n^3 - 5n + 10)$
30. $8x^2(x^2 - x + 1)$
31. $8x(x^4 + 2y^2 + 4)$
32. $8y(3y^2 + 8x + 3)$
33. $9n(-4n^3 + 7m^2 + 9n)$
34. $x(3x^2 + 3xy + 5)$
35. $4x(-3y - 2x + 8)$
36. $10(y^3 - 3x + 7x^2y)$
37. $6n^3(m^4n - 6mn^3 + 8)$
38. $7(-2y + 5 + 4x)$
39. $6(xy - 8y - 4)$
40. $7a^2b^3(9a^2 + 7b + 9)$
41. $(3b + 1)(3b - 1)$
42. $(2b + 1)(2b - 1)$
43. $(5b + 1)(5b - 1)$
44. $(4n + 3)(4n - 3)$
45. $(x + 4)(x - 4)$
46. $(n + 2)(n - 2)$
47. $(4x + 5)(4x - 5)$
48. $(5r + 4)(5r - 4)$
49. $(5x + 2)(5x - 2)$
50. $(x + 1)(x - 1)$
51. $(3n - 2)2$
52. $(x - 1)2$
53. $(x + 1)2$
54. $(3x - 5)2$
55. $(3k + 1)2$
56. $(5p + 3)2$
57. $(4n - 3)2$
58. $(4m + 5)2$
59. $(x + 4)2$
60. $(k + 3)2$

Page 49: Standard Linear Equations

1. 8
2. -10
3. -8
4. 3
5. -2
6. 0
7. 5
8. -1
9. -3
10. 1
11. -7
12. -6
13. -1
14. -5
15. 8
16. -10
17. 8
18. -3
19. 3
20. 10
21. -9
22. 1
23. -7
24. 0
25. -3
26. -8
27. -9
28. -2
29. 4
30. -7
31. 8
32. -2
33. 5
34. -10
35. 5
36. 8
37. -7
38. -4
39. 9
40. -4

Page 54: Find Slope from Two Points

1. 6	7. 9	13. 9	19. 6	25. -7
2. -6	8. -4	14. -5	20. 9	26. -4
3. -5	9. 7	15. -4	21. 4	27. -4
4. 4	10. -3	16. -1	22. -6	28. -10
5. 9	11. -5	17. 7	23. -8	29. 1
6. 5	12. -3	18. -1	24. 5	30. 5

Page 58: Quadratic Equations

1. (2.062, -2.062)	21. (2, -1.8)	41. (-1.153, 2.278)	61. No real solution.
2. (-6, 6)	22. (1.782, -1.924)	42. (-1.772, 0.439)	62. (-1.5, 1)
3. (-2, -0.5)	23. (-0.603, 0.603)	43. (-0.783, -10.217)	63. No real solution.
4. (-4, 5.167)	24. (-1)	44. (1.149, -1.524)	64. (0.612, -0.612)
5. (-4.458, 1.458)	25. (2.833, -2)	45. (1, 0.4)	65. (1.198, -1.531)
6. (-8, 14)	26. No real solution.	46. (8, -3)	66. (3, -9)
7. (0.588, -1.7)	27. (12, -12)	47. (-1.581, 1.581)	67. (1.065, -1.792)
8. (1.467, -1.753)	28. (2, 1.667)	48. (-1.531, 6.531)	68. (3.5, -3)
9. (-1.667, -2)	29. (-2.449, 2.449)	49. (-0.531, 1.131)	69. (-3.5, 3.5)
10. No real solution.	30. (7, -4.5)	50. No real solution.	70. (-5, 3)
11. (4.5, -5.333)	31. (1.4, -3)	51. (4.541, -1.541)	71. (-0.69, 0.29)
12. (1.232, -0.959)	32. No real solution.	52. (5.833, -4)	72. (0.6, -2)
13. (-6.25, 5)	33. (-1.221, 1.721)	53. (-3, 0.75)	73. (-0.553, 0.678)
14. (-6, 7.667)	34. (1.667, -2.5)	54. (0.914, -1.914)	74. (14, -9)
15. (2.327, -1.827)	35. (-4, 1)	55. (0.757, -1.057)	75. (2.553, -0.839)
16. (-0.368, -1.632)	36. (-8, 8)	56. (4.667, -1)	76. (2.5, -7)
17. (1.138, 0.195)	37. (-0.5, -0.333)	57. No real solution.	77. (4.899, -4.899)
18. (4, -4)	38. (-2.12, 1.029)	58. (-1, 5)	78. (2.958, -0.958)
19. (2.387, 0.279)	39. (-3.333, 7)	59. (4.782, -1.115)	79. (-4.4, 5)
20. (-2.052, 0.766)	40. (-0.929, 1.829)	60. (1.826, -1.826)	80. (-3, -0.5)

81. (5, -7)
82. (-0.613, -2.721)
83. No real solution.
84. (1.869, -0.869)
85. (1.063, -1.646)

86. (-0.36, 0.694)
87. (4.294, -2.794)
88. (4, -5.333)
89. (14, -4)
90. (-0.676, 1.776)

91. (-3, 1.333)
92. (-1.525, 0.525)
93. (-1, 1)
94. (3.676, -2.176)
95. (1.155, -1.155)

96. (3.5, -5.333)
97. No real solution.
98. No real solution.
99. (6, -6)
100. (-1.648, 1.648)

Page 71: Polynomials: Addition and Subtraction

1. $13m^3 - 3m^2$
2. $6k^4 + 13k$
3. $8v^3 + 8v^2$
4. $3x^4 + 12x + 4$
5. $7n^4 - n^3$
6. $p^3 + 11 p^2$
7. $3b^4 + 13$
8. $9k^3 + 5k^2$
9. $6a - 1$
10. $4r^3 + 7r + 10$
11. $9n^4 + 7n$
12. $11a - 4$
13. -4
14. $-4x^3 + 2x^2$
15. $5k^2 - 2k + 15$
16. $-n^2 + 7$
17. $-7x^4 + 4$
18. $8a^4 + a^3$
19. $11 p^4 - 5 p^3$
20. $4n^2 - 3$
21. $-14a^4 + 2a^2$
22. $3n^3 + 7n$
23. $6v^2 - 9$
24. $-2x$
25. $3x^3 + 6$
26. $-2n^2 + 2n$
27. $-3 p^4 + 4 p$
28. $4x^3 - 1$
29. $13r^3 + 10r^2$
30. $-3b^4 - 4b^2$

31. $-2x^3 + x^2 + 12$
32. $6n^4 + 5n - 5$
33. $-13n^4 - 3n^2 + 14$
34. $3x^4 + 2x^3 + x^2$
35. $4n^4 + 10n^3 - 2n^2$
36. $9v^3 - v^2 + 8v$
37. $-3p^3 - 5p^2 + 4$
38. $-k^4 - 5k^2 + k$
39. $10x^2 - 3x - 4$
40. $-6k^4 - k^3 + 9$
41. $a^3 - 7a^2 + 4a$
42. $-4x^3 + 9x^2 - 5x$
43. $8x^4 + 5x + 10$
44. $-2x^3 - 8x^2 + 11x$
45. $7x^3 - 5x^2 - 5x$
46. $-8x^3 + 11x^2 + 10$
47. $-5x^3 + 8x^2 + 14$
48. $-4x^4 - 2x^3 - 8x$
49. $9n^3 + 2n - 2$
50. $-a^4 + 4a^3 + 5a^2$
51. $10x^4 - 6x^3 - 5$
52. $-8a^4 + 11a^2 + 4$
53. $-12x^2 + 7x - 2$
54. $11x^2 - 8x$
55. $5n^4 - 6n^2 + 6$
56. $-5k^3 + 5k^2 + 9k$
57. $-2x^3 + 7x^2 - 7x$
58. $5n^4 - 4n^3 + 13n^2$
59. $-5v^3 + 8v^2 + 15$
60. $-4b^4 + 10b^3 + b$

61. $2a^3 + 3a^2 - 1$
62. $-2a^4 + 8a^3 + 5a^2$
63. $5a^3 + 5a^2 - 4$
64. $14x^4 - 2x^3 + 10x + 6$
65. $2 p^4 + 7 p^2 - 4 p$
66. $-3x^4 + 8x^3 - 9x^2 + 7x$
67. $5v^4 + v^3 + v + 3$
68. $4 p^3 + 9 p + 12$
69. $3x^4 + 9x$
70. $2x^3 - 13x^2 - 5x + 7$
71. $15n^4 + 14n^3 - 11$
72. $-4v^3 + 4v^2 + 13v$
73. $3v^3 + 4v^2 - 7v$
74. $4n^3 - 11n + 4$
75. $11v^3 - 2v^2 + v - 3$
76. $-3n^3 - 5n^2 + 10n - 7$
77. $4x^4 + 10x^3 - x - 5$
78. $15x^4 + x^2 - 7x$
79. $3x^4 - 7x^2 - x$
80. $5n^4 + 3n^3 - 3n$
81. $-4 p^4 - 2 p^3 - p - 4$
82. $7v^4 - 5v - 9$
83. $-14p^4 + 4p^3 + 11p^2 - 7$
84. $7n^4 - 5n^3 + n + 1$
85. $3v^3 - v^2 + 6$
86. $7x^2 + 5x + 11$
87. $n^2 + 6n$
88. $-7a^4 + 10a^3 + 6a + 2$
89. $-3b^4 - 3b + 1$
90. $-2x^3 + 8x^2 + 2x + 7$

Page 83: Polynomials: Multiplication

1. $10x^2 + 6xy - 28y^2$
2. $5a^2 - 15ab + 10b^2$
3. $7x^2 - 40xy - 12y^2$
4. $32a^2 - 32ab + 8b^2$
5. $8x^2 - 47xy + 35y^2$
6. $4u^2 + 16uv + 12v^2$
7. $25x^2 + 15xy - 4y^2$
8. $3a^2 - 27ab + 42b^2$
9. $35a^2 - 77ab + 42b^2$
10. $42x^2 - 63xy + 21y^2$
11. $28x^2 + 39xy + 8y^2$
12. $6m^2 + 53mn + 40n^2$
13. $14a^2 + 48ab + 18b^2$
14. $48x^2 + 10xy - 3y^2$
15. $12x^2 + 12xy - 9y^2$
16. $16a^2 + 40ab + 16b^2$
17. $4x^2 - 19xy - 30y^2$
18. $10a^2 - 11ab - 35b^2$
19. $6a^2 + 11ab + 3b^2$
20. $35x^2 - 51xy + 18y^2$
21. $2x^2 - 8y^2$
22. $30a^2 - 9ab - 12b^2$
23. $40x^2 - 70xy + 30y^2$
24. $40m^2 - 5mn - 35n^2$
25. $2u^2 + 2uv - 4v^2$
26. $30x^2 + 27xy + 6y^2$
27. $15x^2 + 56xy + 49y^2$
28. $16x^2 - 70xy + 24y^2$
29. $24x^2 - 20xy - 16y^2$
30. $15x^2 + 8xy - 12y^2$
31. $20u^3 - 11u^2v - 67uv^2 - 30v^3$
32. $3x^3 + 19x^2y + 4xy^2 - 12y^3$
33. $49a^3 - 63a^2b + 15ab^2 - 8b^3$
34. $36a^3 - 72a^2b + 74ab^2 - 28b^3$
35. $42u^3 - 32u^2v - 36uv^2 + 14v^3$
36. $4x^3 - 2xy^2 - 2y^3$
37. $35u^3 + 2u^2v + 9uv^2 + 2v^3$
38. $24x^3 + 43x^2y - 8xy^2 - 42y^3$
39. $m^3 - m^2n - 4mn^2 - 32n^3$
40. $4a^3 + 38a^2b + 36ab^2 - 18b^3$
41. $16x^3 - 20x^2y + 24xy^2 + 36y^3$
42. $30x^3 + 18x^2y - 13xy^2 + 56y^3$
43. $40m^3 + 17m^2n - 10mn^2 + n^3$
44. $5x^3 - 41x^2y + 17xy^2 + 30y^3$
45. $32x^3 - 24x^2y + 12xy^2 - 40y^3$
46. $42x^3 - 48x^2y + 36xy^2 - 30y^3$
47. $6u^3 - 31u^2v + 50uv^2 - 25v^3$
48. $21a^3 - 14a^2b + 5ab^2 + 4b^3$
49. $49x^3 - 49x^2y + 61xy^2 - 21y^3$
50. $12x^3 + 25x^2y + 16xy^2 + 3y^3$
51. $24m^3 + 2m^2n - 8mn^2 - 2n^3$
52. $8x^3 - 26x^2y + 8xy^2 - 6y^3$
53. $7x^3 + 22x^2y + 18xy^2 + 4y^3$
54. $35m^3 - 44m^2n - 23mn^2 + 14n^3$
55. $20x^3 - 5x^2y - 25xy^2 + 10y^3$
56. $10x^3 - x^2y - 13xy^2 - 12y^3$
57. $2x^3 - 7x^2y - 20xy^2 - 8y^3$
58. $20a^3 - 42a^2b + 22ab^2 - 6b^3$
59. $42a^3 + 78a^2b - 13ab^2 - 42b^3$
60. $16x^3 + 16x^2y - 16xy^2 - 6y^3$
61. $56x^4 + 96x^3y + 5x^2y^2 - 41xy^3 - 21y^4$
62. $24x^4 - 6x^3y - 88x^2y^2 - 42xy^3 + 16y^4$
63. $24a^4 + 58a^3b + 67a^2b^2 + 47ab^3 + 14b^4$
64. $6x^4 - 35x^3y + 51x^2y^2 + 14xy^3 - 48y^4$
65. $42u^4 - 13u^3v - 57u^2v^2 - 28uv^3 - 4v^4$
66. $6u^4 + 8u^3v + 11u^2v^2 + 25uv^3 + 25v^4$
67. $21a^4 - 35a^3b - 100a^2b^2 - 88ab^3 - 32b^4$
68. $14m^4 + 9m^3n - 17m^2n^2 - 7mn^3 + n^4$
69. $35m^4 + 8m^3n - 73m^2n^2 + 12mn^3 + 18n^4$
70. $24x^4 - 16x^3y - 63x^2y^2 + 35xy^3 + 25y^4$
71. $25u^4 - 5u^3v - 40u^2v^2 - 76uv^3 - 48v^4$
72. $4u^4 - 18u^3v - 2u^2v^2 - 2uv^3 - 6v^4$
73. $12x^4 + 11x^2y^2 - 23xy^3 - 40y^4$
74. $12x^4 + 46x^3y - 28x^2y^2 - 30xy^3 + 8y^4$
75. $6x^4 - 38x^3y - 48x^2y^2 + 2xy^3 + 6y^4$
76. $36x^4 - 24x^3y + 7x^2y^2 - 16xy^3 - 3y^4$
77. $3x^4 - 19x^3y + 3x^2y^2 - 16xy^3 - 6y^4$
78. $15x^4 + 46x^2y^2 - 19xy^3 + 56y^4$
79. $12u^4 - 37u^3v + 35u^2v^2 - 21uv^3 - 49v^4$
80. $21x^4 + 29x^3y + 23x^2y^2 - 27xy^3 - 18y^4$
81. $6x^4 - 25x^3y - 32x^2y^2 - 17xy^3 - 42y^4$
82. $8a^4 - 6a^2b^2 - 18ab^3 - 10b^4$

83. $5a^4 - 27a^3b - 19ab^3 - 15b^4$
84. $8m^4 - 10m^3n + m^2n^2 - 5mn^3 + 2n^4$
85. $30x^4 + 26x^3y + 17x^2y^2 + 44xy^3 - 7y^4$
86. $56m^4 - 14m^3n - 154m^2n^2 + 14mn^3 + 56n^4$

87. $2x^4 - 10x^3y + 9x^2y^2 + 4xy^3 - 5y^4$
88. $64x^4 - 72x^3y + 80x^2y^2 - 58xy^3 + 14y^4$
89. $12x^4 - 28x^3y - 89x^2y^2 + 28xy^3 + 32y^4$
90. $24a^4 - 4a^3b - 43a^2b^2 + 27ab^3 - 18b^4$